DO I WANT TO BE A MOM?

A Woman's Guide to the Decision of a Lifetime

DIANA L. DELL, M.D., FACOG, AND SUZAN EREM

Contemporary Books

Chicago   New York   San Francisco   Lisbon   London   Madrid   Mexico City
Milan   New Delhi   San Juan   Seoul   Singapore   Sydney   Toronto

The *McGraw-Hill* Companies

Library of Congress Cataloging-in-Publication Data

Dell, Diana L.
    Do I want to be a mom? : a woman's guide to the decision of a lifetime / Diana Dell
and Suzan Erem.
        p.   cm.
    Includes bibliographical references and index.
    ISBN 0-07-140074-5
        1. Motherhood.   2. Mother and child.   3. Working mothers.   I. Erem, Suzan.
II. Title.

HQ759.D438   2003
306.874'3—dc21   2003043981

1 2 3 4 5 6 7 8 9 0   DOC/DOC   2 1 0 9 8 7 6 5 4 3

ISBN 0-07-140074-5

McGraw-Hill books are available at special quantity discounts to use as premiums and sales
promotions, or for use in corporate training programs. For more information, please write to
the Director of Special Sales, Professional Publishing, McGraw-Hill, Two Penn Plaza, New York,
NY 10121-2298. Or contact your local bookstore.

This book is printed on acid-free paper.

To my amazing daugher, Ayshe. May every woman who takes the leap into motherhood be so lucky to end up with a daughter like you.
—Suzan Erem

To my own mother; may she rest in peace.
—Diana Dell

Contents

1 Our Instincts, Goals, and Conflicts   1

2   Age Matters   31

3   Why Am I Worried?   49

8 How Will Children Affect My Career?

9 What Does It Cost to Have and Raise Children?

Preface

Momentous decisions in most women's lives are made (sometimes quite literally) in the dark. We can't always see all the choices available. We don't always know what's right for us. We can't always predict how things will turn out. This book will cast a small glow on the one decision that stays with a woman for her entire lifetime: the decision whether or not to have children.

That illumination comes from the voices of women who have told us their stories. They responded to questions that many women have about motherhood but are afraid to ask: What will it do to my career? What will it do to my body and my health? How will it affect my marriage? Can I afford to raise and educate a child? How much time does it take? Could a child really love me? How can I find the courage to say I don't want children? How long can I wait before I really have to decide? What if I decide not to have kids?

The World Health Organization estimates there are 200 to 225 million pregnancies around the world every year. A full one-third of the pregnancies—seventy-five million—are unwanted, according to Family Care International and the Safe Motherhood Inter-Agency Group. A separate study by the highly respected Alan Guttmacher Institute concluded that 38 percent of pregnancies are unintentional, and that annually, 22 percent of these end in abortion. That study also estimates that in Eastern Europe, 63 percent of pregnancies are unintentional; in Latin America, 52 percent; and in North America, New Zealand, Australia, and Japan, around 45 percent.

In the United States, women will give birth to more than four million babies this year—for a few hundred thousand different reasons. Most of those babies will be brought into this world with intent. Others will not be. At the time of conception, half of all pregnancies are unplanned. Most of these unplanned pregnancies are simply mistimed, but 15 to 18 percent will result in children who are unwanted—also for a few hundred thousand different reasons. And another important statistic has been emerging over the past twenty-five years: the number of U.S. women not having children at all has nearly doubled.

But if you are wondering about whether or not to become a mother, then only one question begins your journey: will I be happier with children or without them?

SUZAN'S STORY

My mother was a bipolar alcoholic whose untreated illnesses created a lot of misery in my childhood. In 1986, when I was twenty-two, I became pregnant. Fearing I would turn out like my mother, I ended the pregnancy and never once regretted it.

Within a year after my marriage to the man with whom I first became pregnant, birth control failed again. I told my husband I still didn't want to have children because I was convinced I would never be a good mother. I offered him an amicable divorce so he could find someone who wanted children. He turned me down. I was still young, he said. There was plenty of time. I had my second abortion and continued to build my career.

During our years together, the question of whether or not we would have children turned very subtly into *when* we would have children. When we had been together seven years, I was twenty-nine years old and between jobs. We were in a new city. My father was terminally ill. My husband was gainfully employed. I decided this time made the most sense.

When I admitted to my gynecologist that I was afraid of motherhood, the only book she could recommend was *What to Expect When You're Expecting*. It just didn't fit the bill.

After six months of trying, I got pregnant, and nine months later gave birth to a beautiful, bright little girl with a strong personality and a caring nature. I worried every day that I'd fail at motherhood.

I had not been able to foresee the pressures of work and home, of no family support, of a new city, and of a husband whose job pulled him away from home frequently. Eventually, driven by depression, a lack of role models, and a deteriorating marriage, I faced the most desperate of choices. I decided I could be a better mother from a distance and moved out of the house.

As my daughter grows, I stay very involved in her life and have become much more confident as a mom. We fall in love over and over again, having "ticklefests" and "dirty-sock fights," cuddling on the sofa, or talking quietly about God, schoolwork, and girlfriends. Many moms report the same experience, that every day their children provide an endless source of joy and laughter, personal challenge, and growth. The only difference is that I don't *see* my daughter every day, and there are times that makes us both very sad.

My story isn't all that uncommon, but it is unspoken. More than two million families in this country are headed by single men, a sign that many people no longer assume that only mothers can raise children well. Talk-show host Oprah Winfrey said her solicitation to viewers for a 2002 show on mothers who were surprised by the challenges of motherhood received the biggest response she had ever received in eighteen years of doing her show.

DIANA'S STORY

As I look back over my life, I cannot recall ever thinking, "When I have children of my own . . . ," as I planned what I would do with my life. I never made an active, conscious decision not to have children. But as I moved through adulthood, career joys and obligations were far ahead of any imagined family or children joys. My career remains my most cherished endeavor.

But as a professional woman moving into and through my forties, I came to believe that women like me often feel driven to be creative in other ways—as though women with children have already created a living memorial to their lives that I did not have.

I am a nurturing person who loves puppies and children and finds herself drawn to both in social encounters. I fondly recall how happy it made me to interact with the babies I brought into this world as moms came back to my obstetrical clinic over time. But I have to chuckle as I recall that it made me equally happy to hand them back to their parents. Over my long professional career, I have cared for thousands of childbearing women. I have shared their joys and sorrows, with no real contemplation that this was a journey I needed to make myself in order to be fulfilled. I have no regrets.

In my work as both an obstetrician-gynecologist and a psychiatrist, I am increasingly aware that modern life has moved having children from an automatic, biologically driven process to a highly complex psychological and social issue. And making the "wrong" decision in either direction can profoundly affect the physical and mental health of a woman and her loved ones. That is why we wrote this book.

THIS BOOK

We interviewed, surveyed, and talked with women from all walks of life, a range of ethnic backgrounds, and every region of the country. You'll hear comments from pregnant women, new moms, veteran moms, and empty nesters. You'll also hear from women who never had the desire for children, and those who wanted children but couldn't have them. While we've changed the names of the women we spoke with, we haven't changed their stories.

We raise the questions and give you the information you need to consider—the cost, the network of people available to help you raise children, and the effects on your relationship, career, and spirit. We let the women who've been there tell their stories, while providing you the framework within which to examine your motivations and make your choice.

The book is organized so that you can turn directly to the section that addresses your issues, bounce around to different sections, or read it from beginning to end. But mostly we hope that as you read this book, however you read it, it will light your path toward the most momentous decision you'll ever make.

Acknowledgments

We jointly thank first the hundreds of women we interviewed, surveyed, and talked with, who told their stories with such candor and generosity. Without you, this book would not exist. We also thank our agent, Caroline Carney, for her tireless proposal editing; our editor, Judith McCarthy, for grace under pressure; and our production editor, Ellen Vinz, for getting the job done.

Diana thanks Khris Sherlock, Carolyn Haynes, and Phyllis Dye, each of whom helps in her own way to make projects like this possible—both when Diana is at Duke and when she is away. She also thanks the hundreds of women who have shared their stories and their wisdom over the past thirty years in her nursing and medical practices.

Suzan (suzan@lastdraft.com) thanks the early supporters of the project, including Sally Faith Dorfman, Karen Kubby, Pat Ernenwein, Nancy Burgoyne, Jill Vibhakar, Lori Erickson, Paul Ingram, Gail Messenger, Susan Johnson, Caroline Downs, Katharine Assante, Effie Mihopoulos, Karen Ford, Pat Badtke, Kay Irelan, Jeanne Stokes, and Lucia Valenska. Thanks to fellow National Writers Union member Jeannette Cézanne for her diligent fact checking. Thanks to the staff of the Java House at Prairie Lights for letting her overstay her welcome and to the Iowa City *Press-Citizen* for understanding why she had to leave so soon. Thanks always to her partner and best friend, Paul Durrenberger. Finally, thank you to the woman who was there from the start, who always provided invaluable feedback and support every step of the way—Kate Gleeson, an exceptional writer and even more exceptional friend.

Introduction

Beginning early in our lives, most women have a running dialogue with ourselves about having children. We don't all recognize it for what it is, but this dialogue—in our minds and among our friends—stays with us, emerging throughout our youth, getting louder in late adolescence, becoming a steady hum often shared with our lovers during our twenties and thirties, and ending as either a comfortable chat over coffee or a resentful bickering with ourselves in our later years.

Do I want to be a mother? Would I be a good mother? Will I regret it if I don't have children? Which choice will make me the happiest? These are the questions that some of us answer easily and others agonize over. For those who haven't found easy answers, we have written this book. It may appear we are trying to oversimplify your motherhood decision. We aren't. This is the most personal of decisions and will, of course, remain so. What we hope to do is to share the voices of women who have given us their honest, unvarnished thoughts on the issue. We'll address the concerns and fears that many women have raised, as well as the reasons women consider motherhood—the love, fun, and fulfillment that many women gain as mothers.

For many of us, simply having a real choice about motherhood is revolutionary. Our mothers' generation, for the most part, was the first generation with access to birth control throughout its reproductive years. Because of that newness, our moms may not have perceived many other life options. There are, of course, exceptions, but it's the newness of having the power to decide that makes the decision even tougher, as does the pull of career opportunity, economic necessity, or both.

To begin writing, we explored the sources of women's desires to have children or not have children. We asked women why they felt the way they did about motherhood and when they first felt that way. This will help us understand where each of us begins to have this dialogue about children.

I ALWAYS ASSUMED I'D HAVE CHILDREN.

Many women operate all their lives under the basic assumption that they will have children. Part of this attitude stems from what some call our "pro-motherhood society," one in which every woman assumes she'll have children because "it's the thing to do."

> *I don't think I ever sat down and said, "Oh, I want to be a mom." I just knew that at some point in my life, I'd be a mother. I always envisioned myself with kids.*
>
> —PORTIA

> *I always assumed I would have kids, because that's what women did. Every woman in our family had kids—my aunts, my mom. I never thought of not having them until after I had them. I never thought it was an option not to.*
>
> —JILLIAN

In most cases, women with these assumptions went ahead and had children. There was still a trade-off there, because there are times when a woman looks back and wonders what the other life might have been like. Making a conscious decision helps reduce the appeal of that other path.

I NEVER WANTED CHILDREN.

Some women who never saw themselves as mothers had children anyway, for any number of reasons. Some are pleasantly surprised to discover they've grown into a desire for children, whether by an unplanned pregnancy, falling in love, or simply growing older and gaining a new perspective. Others became resigned to the notion that children were an inevitable part of their future, by unplanned pregnancy or simply because it seemed less complicated than the option not to have children. Finally, of course, there are women who knew they never wanted children and didn't have them.

> *I didn't really think I wanted children. I was afraid of childbirth. Family lore was that my mother broke some of her lower vertebrae when she gave birth. So childbirth was terrifying to me. In retrospect, after having my daughter, I wouldn't have wanted to go through life without this experience. It forces you to grow and deal with your own childhood. It expands you.*
>
> —ELLA

> *I never knew that I wanted children. They never entered my head until I had them. I'm Catholic. This was over thirty years ago. We had to get married to have sex, you know. I got married, and we weren't allowed to do anything to prevent pregnancy. Raising them was the happiest time of my life.*
>
> —BERNICE

> *My plans now are to have my children grow up and move out, and to enjoy what I have left of myself and my life. I'll work till I am forced to retire.*
>
> —JEAN

Among women who choose not to have children are those who, later in their lives, examine their childhoods and point to a particular dynamic that turned them off to motherhood. Others had fine childhoods but are comfortable with the notion that children just aren't for them and that they have other things they want to do with their lives.

> *At thirty-eight, I still get comments, mostly from extended family and teenagers. "Isn't it about time you have some kids of your own?" "You'd make a great mom." I probably would make a great mom in some ways, but at the same time I didn't want to make the compromises necessary to be a great mom. I would've had to change my job. I was running a program for*

*homeless teenagers—getting out of bed in the middle of the
night, working late hours, dealing with some pretty rotten
behavior—and I'd come home stressed out.*

—ELIZABETH

*I graduated high school in 1974, post–Vietnam War. I won-
dered about the condition of the world I would bring this baby
into. And I've always been very interested in animals. I always
found it ironic that people focused so carefully about breeding
programs for animals but just anyone could go out and have
kids.*

—JOSIE

The women who know from the start *why* they didn't want children
tend to be at peace when they attend family gatherings without children
of their own or watch their friends play with their grandchildren.

I DIDN'T THINK SERIOUSLY ABOUT IT UNTIL I WAS OLDER.

Many women are highly ambivalent about the motherhood decision. That
ambivalence may keep you from "thinking about it" while you attend to
more immediate issues such as your higher education and early career
choices. That same ambivalence may also delay serious love interests
until you're in your late twenties or early thirties. If you marry, the question "When are you going to have a baby?" may begin to confront you
on a daily basis.

In general, women who aren't thinking about motherhood have lives
where the primary focus is separate from children. "Thinking about it"
would, in fact, mean deciding to alter the direction of that life.

*I don't think I really wanted kids a lot until I was thirty-five.
My ob/gyn prompted me some on that. At thirty-five the "clock
is ticking" as they say, and there just isn't that much time left.
When I was growing up, the emphasis was much more on
getting an education. I was told, "Don't get married until you*

have a college degree. Get your education so you can take care of yourself no matter what."

—SARA

Somehow, in the twenty-two years I've been a lawyer, I got tied to waking up in the morning, putting on a suit, and coming to work. Now that I have a child, I go home early on Wednesdays. The six hours I spend with my little girl are very uncomfortable. Until recently, I'd find myself telling the UPS guy, "I'm really a lawyer, I'm just home because . . . ," and he'd be backing away from me.

—TAMARA

By their midthirties, some women who haven't found a life partner consider single motherhood—an even more radical departure from the lives their mothers led.

My parents didn't take my choice to be a single mother too well, I think because I'm an only child. Personally, I was most concerned about how I'd support a child on my own. I couldn't really look forward to early retirement or that kind of thing. I've enjoyed traveling in my life and figured that certainly was going to change, which it has.

—SHAWN

Each decision—whether it be about what job to take, what person to date, or where to live—creates its own trajectory. Assessing your decisions along the way helps you change direction more easily, as you weigh each choice before you.

I WAS AMBIVALENT UNTIL WE TRIED AND COULDN'T HAVE THEM.

For many women, infertility tends to sharpen the desire for children. So a woman who discovers that she can't conceive loses her ambivalence, and having a baby becomes the most important goal in her life. She feels a loss of control in a life she thought she had under control. She feels robbed of the one thing she always assumed she could do. Others faced with the same challenge come to realize that the life they have without children is OK and probably the life they've wanted all along.

> At twenty-eight, some kind of bizarre hormonal thing went into effect, and I went into this baby frenzy. After two years, I miscarried. About a year later, I lost a baby. Then after another couple of years—doing the whole thing with the temperature and the charts, my husband got shots to boost his sperm—still nothing worked. All of this was taking a toll on us . . . We decided it was time to find something else to do with our lives. Then at age thirty-five, that light switch went off again, and all that baby lust was gone.
>
> —BONNIE

> It was a traumatic period. I had to finally give up on having a baby. Everything I had ever wanted along the way was possible through hard work, and I was able to achieve it. I just refused to believe I would not have this, that it had nothing to do with hard work. I had to let go of it. I wasn't ready to talk about adoption, but my husband thought I should.
>
> —JACQUELINE

I NEVER WANTED KIDS UNTIL I WANTED OUR CHILD.

Finally, the great mystery of life is that we never know what's coming around the corner. We can plan. We can make decisions based on those plans. We can set a course. Then suddenly we fall in love and realize for the first time that for us, children will be the ultimate expression of that love. Or we get the job opportunity to travel the world and consciously decide that isn't the life for children.

Many women who are ambivalent or indifferent about children most of their lives express awe and amazement at the fact that once they met the love of their lives, they suddenly wanted a child. Having a child can be the most intimate, exciting time for a couple, an event that nurtures and breathes even more life into the love they feel for each other. Some couples feel a renewed sense of passion and desire for one another in the realization that their lovemaking will create an entirely new and different human being who carries some of both of them, and whom they see as a manifestation of their eternal love.

> *When I was a kid, I didn't think about having children, but*
> *when I started dating Bob and then married him, I started*
> *thinking about it more seriously. That's when it became real.*
> *I wanted to have a baby with him.*
>
> —MONA

MOVING FORWARD FROM OUR PAST

No one can ever fully predict what the motherhood experience will be like for any woman, but these shared voices can help you see how having or not having children affected other women. With some of the possibilities in mind, you can make as informed a choice as possible and head down the path that's best for you.

Finally, let that quiet dialogue you've been having all your life come to the surface. Express it to people you trust. Talk to yourself out loud. Talk to other women who wavered, and ask them how they feel about their ultimate decision. Weigh the pros and cons, and look critically at your motivations about children. Be sure those motivations are yours, those of the person you have become, before making your decision. Appreciate that you may change your mind as circumstances change and as you grow older, but carefully think through all aspects of this momentous, life-changing decision. In the end, you're likely to be happier with the choice you make.

1

Our Instincts, Goals, and Conflicts

Why do you want a child or want to be child-free? On both sides of the decision are many healthy reasons—meaning reasons that will sustain you through the tough times and keep you content in your old age. There are also unhealthy reasons, ones that could cause a lifetime of disappointment in yourself and with your child, if you decide to have one.

Biological drive, family life, cultural influence, personal needs, religious background, and romantic love all contribute to a woman's desire to become a mother. These influences can be conscious or unconscious, and most of them have a profound effect on us long before we ever deliberately think about the motherhood decision.

It's Basic Biology.

As we grow into puberty, we experience a powerful interest in exploring sex. It is this purely biological drive that explains why teens begin experimenting with sex against all common sense, fear of sexually transmitted diseases, parental warnings, and educational films at school. Besides, for most of us, sex feels good, and that helps ensure the continuation of our species.

Being pregnant is fun and exciting for many women as well. Your body begins to change almost immediately. Many women describe the experience of creating a life and having a person growing inside them as the beginning of the miracle they have always heard about. Pregnant women also tend to get a lot of positive attention. They feel special and often enjoy a sense of happy anticipation (once the morning sickness wears off!).

> *I had the sense inside of me that something was ready to explode positively, like there was a caged bird inside of me that wanted to sing.*
>
> —EMMA

> *The social approbation was like nothing I'd ever experienced. I liked being the center of attention; I liked buying all new clothes. I have one of the world's best career maternity wardrobes. I liked presenting cases in court pregnant. I liked having elevators held for me.*
>
> —LANA

I Want to Carry On My Family.

Our family of origin and a desire to carry it on play a huge role in many women's decisions about motherhood.

Most of us still have a strong sense of family, despite physical distances between family members and the inevitable stresses between generations. Family gives us a touchstone in the bigger world, a place to belong and a place to escape if necessary. Family is the biggest part of our personal history for the first twenty years of our lives, and strong family bonds can be one of the greatest motivations for much of what we do later in life.

> We're all very close. I can say now that whatever would happen in my life, I could call on any cousin anytime, and maybe we don't talk a lot, but if I need something, I'd get that help, that backup that family should do for you.
>
> —ROCHELLE

> It became increasingly difficult for me in my thirties to be around all of my cousins, who got married around then, when we'd get together for reunions. It was really painful to me. My sister, who's younger than me, had several kids. I wasn't anywhere near ready to do that.
>
> —TULA

Our culture, like our biological drive, strongly fosters the notion of passing on the family genes. Family members and friends lovingly coo and cluck over a baby's features by attributing one or another to someone in the previous generation. "He has your nose," and "She has your eyes," are common compliments. The parents beam at the knowledge they've passed on a piece of themselves to their child. It's also fascinating to see how you and your partner's genes come together in this new person you've created.

Adoptive parents, who sometimes get the same comments from unsuspecting adults, can relish the way their child imitates their figures of speech or hand motions. In their early years, genes aren't the only factor in how children look; they mimic facial expressions and posture, so they actually do look like the adoptive parents.

In both cases, parents enjoy a sense of immortality, knowing that once they are gone, a part of them lives on.

We Have Such Great Traditions.

Women who are strongly influenced by family often cite a desire to carry on family traditions. We want to relive the positive experiences of our childhood, and re-create the wonderful parenting our mothers did. Many aim to do it even better. We may have a family farm or business we hope to pass on to the next generation, or we just want to continue the simple traditions of Sunday dinners, birthday parties, and pumpkin picking.

Knowledge of our traditions provides an immense sense of security and fulfillment to women who have children. We become the experts in our own family about decorating a tree, lighting a menorah, or organizing the family reunion. These traditions, and the expertise of carrying them out, provide a safe, strong network of loving people to comfort a child. They also provide a feeling of competence and dignity for the mother.

> In my family, autumn was the best season. We would all carve
> pumpkins out on the front porch. Then we'd come inside,
> where my mom had a hot meal waiting for us, served in little
> pumpkins. The dining room would be decked out in candles
> and fall decorations. So I do what I can to re-create that for my
> family. I think it's a magical time of year.
>
> —CELIA

My Family Wants Me to Have Children.

It isn't unusual for a mother or well-meaning relatives at family gatherings to ask a woman in her twenties when she will "settle down and have children." Most young women are spared this until they have at least introduced a serious love interest to the family, but others hear it more and more as they grow older. Many women face a growing impatience and even a certain audacity from family members who are eagerly awaiting children.

> *When we told my mother that we decided not to do in vitro fertilization, partly because of the expense, she pulled out her checkbook and started writing a check for $30,000 so we'd get three shots at it!*
>
> —CORY

> *When I was thirty and still didn't have babies, I really felt like a freak. My family kept pressuring us. My mother even got on this kick that maybe we should adopt. She openly said, "I don't know why you don't just adopt a kid!"*
>
> —DOROTHY

Many women grew up hearing such conversations at family gatherings, long before those questions or suggestions were aimed at *them*. They also grew up watching other young women in the family marrying and having babies. Like many aspects of the motherhood decision, making your choices independently of family pressure allows you more comfort in your decision in the long run.

For instance, if your family is strong and your traditions trustworthy, you may have the network you need to get critical assistance in raising your children. But when you face challenging times with your baby and your family isn't nearby to assist, you can look back at your decision and realize you made it for yourself, not for others, and that it's up to you to find the solutions that will suit you best.

> *My mom lived out of town. She was busy with her own life. I had to take my baby to the sitter every day. My husband did nothing. I just did what I had to do, minute by minute. I never found time for myself—not then, I didn't.*
>
> —KATHY

I Hope to Heal from My Dysfunctional Childhood.

There's a common dangerous side to how family pressures influence our desire to have children. Many women grew up in difficult or dysfunctional families and want a chance to do it better, healing that pain in the process. Others decide against motherhood because they fear they will repeat their parents' mistakes and feel that putting those experiences behind them is the best way to heal from them. As an adult, you now have the opportunity to see your family, its limitations and its damaging effects, from the perspective of an adult. You have your own life and your own choices ahead of you, and you can make those choices independently of whatever harm befell you as a child.

When women with unhappy childhoods decide to have children because they want to show themselves and others they can do it better, it is possible for them to heal old emotional wounds. The healing starts when they identify an important, although painful, part of themselves.

This decision can also be dangerous. First, children are individuals with their own demands and needs. You may do "everything right" and still have a tough time with a spirited, independent, or difficult child. Second, unless you are guided by a positive role model from outside your immediate family, you probably have only the negative one provided by your mother. Unfortunately, under stress, we all revert to what is most familiar, so we may repeat much of what our parents did, even the most reprehensible things.

I wanted a big family because I came from such a dysfunc-
tional family. I was going to do everything right. The man
I married would love me forever and be the perfect provider.
I got married at age seventeen, had a baby ten months later,
and [had] more after that. In the end, it turned out I couldn't
do it. My husband and I separated, and I let them live with
their dad.

—BOBBI

I tried so hard to raise my daughter differently than I was
raised. It hurts sometimes to see so much of my mother—
and so little of me—in her. But I can't seem to change it. I try
to figure out a way to celebrate it, but sometimes that can
be hard.

—KIRSTEN

For women who feel swayed in their decision for or against having children by a less-than-optimal family history, help is available. Counseling, support groups, parenting books, and parenting skills classes can help you identify your fears and weaknesses and give you the tools you'll need to be a better parent or understand more fully why you don't want children. Doing this kind of psychological work in adulthood will help you define better who you are now, compared with that young, often scared or violated little girl you once were.

It's What Most People Do.

We can feel peer pressure very strongly, even after we reach adulthood. Somehow, as our own friends start having baby showers and shifting identities, many of us start to feel the pull to join them. Within moments of a woman announcing she's pregnant, the people around her begin to offer congratulations, then advice ranging from the best diet during pregnancy to the benefits of breastfeeding.

After the baby is born, the new parents are welcomed into the open arms of other parents, who offer advice and swap stories about how their babies eat, sleep, don't sleep, and change. Suddenly you're earning your way into that community of adults who know what it's like to go months without a solid night's sleep, who discuss things like "poop" and "pee pee" in public and are trying to figure out the best form of discipline.

> *Having friends who have kids, we understand some of the same joys and heartbreaks. You feel closer to them because they understand how easy it is to feel manipulated or why you're having trouble saying no.*
>
> —CARLA

The community of families is a geographical one as well as an emotional one. While many parents find their familiar neighborhood is a network perfectly suitable for raising children, family-friendly, often suburban, communities offer parents a range of child care options, toddler playtimes, storytelling at the local public library, and playgrounds in the neighborhood. While such a community often offers the benefits of living among a network of other young families, finding it could also mean relocating, possibly disrupting work, family relationships, and friendships.

Lastly, while the subtle welcoming pressure of becoming a parent can expand a woman's network of new acquaintances, it doesn't do much to encourage or maintain old friendships, especially with child-free friends. While new moms can easily make new friends with other mothers by striking up conversations about food, sleep, or clothing, child-free friends from "before baby" may still be cruising along in conversations about work, dating, and late nights on the town. This shift can influence child-free friends to desire to join the "mom club" now or someday—or reinforce their lack of desire to talk diapers and doo-doo. At the same time, new mothers may wistfully wonder what they're missing from their "old" life. In any case, the effect of children on friendships can be profound.

When we had kids, the friends we had without children seemed to drift away a little, and the ones with kids became closer. Now that the childless ones are having kids, they are starting to drift back!

—KATY

Be sure you're having a child for the right reasons. Not because "all my friends have one."

—MARIE

I Have the Ability to Create Life.

Having a child offers a woman the joy of creation. Not only does she experience that unparalleled feeling of the fetus growing inside and the actual birth of the child, but the teaching that a parent does from the very first days of a baby's life. Many adoptive parents also experience this surge of creative energy. In both cases, parents, but primarily the mother, are switching roles from a single human being to someone responsible for everything that a young baby will experience (for better or for worse). You will be the interpreter, the translator, and the mediator between your baby and the world. You will encourage, train, educate, and discipline your child in the ways of the world in which you both live. You are helping to form a new personality.

> *From infant to age five, you are everything to this child! It's amazing to see how much they learn in such a short time.*
> —BELINDA

> *The years from five to twelve were a beautiful time. They are cooperative and loving, and they think you walk on water.*
> —KERRI

> *They are wonderful. They help me, make me laugh, keep me even busier than I ever was, give me the excuse to rent movies I always wanted to see and buy books and toys that I love, too!*

*We have mutual interests in our hobbies, and we do a lot
together.*

—ROBIN

While some find creating a life and helping to develop a child's personality the ultimate reward, there's no denying it takes a lot of time.
Women who choose not to have children have more energy and time for
other interests. You can run off to the movies without having to find and
pay a baby-sitter. You can travel the country without the guilt and complications of either leaving your children behind or trying to drag them
along. You can pursue your artistic talents without the worry of the financial pressures of raising a child. You can stay up until the wee hours of
the morning developing medical advances that could save lives, without
worrying about getting the kids off to school by 8:00 A.M.

I May Learn Something About Myself.

Raising children is often a struggle that draws on reserves most women don't know they have until the time comes. Children can be immensely challenging, from the toddler who screams at unimaginable levels at exactly the most embarrassing moment to the teenager who wrecks the car. Experiences along that continuum are awaiting every mother, and you can't always predict whether you have the strength to survive them with your sanity intact. Still, most women come through these difficult experiences and realize later that they were stronger, more patient, and more flexible than they ever thought they could be.

> There were times when my son would start to act out, and then I'd have to say, "Wait a minute, I'm not playing this game with you." Testing and testing and testing. It's exhausting, but that said, it's also wonderful. I'm going to miss it horribly when he moves away.
>
> —PIPER

Then there are women who are disappointed in their ability to mother, who thought they would find that inner strength but didn't. These women tend to be very critical of themselves for not doing a better job with their children. Still, they grow through this painful experience as well.

> It took so much energy. I just didn't have it. I tried, but I just didn't have it. I don't know how other women do it. It'll be a

*long time before my kids understand, and I don't know if
they'll ever forgive me, but I hope some day they do.*

—SANDY

Women who choose not to be mothers also must find immense
strength inside themselves. As many of the topics in this book show,
there's a tidal wave of pressure in our society to have children, and many
child-free women still experience the basic assumption among parents
that if you don't have children, it's because you *can't* have them. The
woman who can state without flinching that she chose not to be a mother
has found great strength within her to face that prejudice.

I Have So Much Love to Give.

In the end, the best motivation for having a child is your desire to love it. To become a content mom, you must always be able to give (emotionally, not necessarily materially) unconditionally to your child, while expecting nothing in return. When your child is free to become whatever he or she will, in the child's own way and own time, with your support and love, without judgment, your child has the highest potential for growing into a healthy adult.

> *I was excited to have my first child, but I wasn't prepared for how intensely I would love him. It was different from my love for my husband or my own parents—it was protective love. I began to understand why animal mothers are the most dangerous creatures if you threaten their offspring.*
>
> *—JANE*

> *You have to be able to provide a home. You have to have the confidence that you can give to your children. You have to be able to sit down with them, give them the time. You have to be willing to sacrifice some of the time you would need for yourself. You have to be prepared to give up a lot of your own dreams if you want to raise a successful child, if you want that child to grow up self-assured.*
>
> *—GINNIE*

Women who choose not to have children must have a strong sense of self-confidence and self-love to know that they are worthy people and complete women. They may choose not to interact with children, find other ways to love children, or find ways that will give back to their community without tying themselves to a role and a responsibility for which they don't feel suited.

I've been to more than my share of ballet recitals and that sort of thing. We get together with nieces and nephews and do some physical stuff, band concerts in the summer, have a picnic; everyone enjoys that. We go swimming together in the summer, ice-skating in the winter. The parents are always grateful for the help, and if you're not going to have kids, you owe it to society to help out. Like it or not, they're your future.

—JAN

Children Are Just Fun!

Children add fun to life. Young children can say the most hilarious things as they learn to put ideas together, and it can be amazing to watch the world through a young child's eyes. Everything is fresh and new. A baby never tires of peekaboo, and a four-year-old who has laughed at your coin or finger trick always wants you to "do it again!" Older children want to play ball or go to a movie with you, and even teens, for all the struggles they endure in adolescence, can brighten your day with an unexpected gift or a kind word.

> *Babies are remarkably social and engaging. I meet many*
> *people, especially elders, through my baby.*
>
> —SHARON

> *I enjoyed carpooling, helping teachers in schools. I baked*
> *cookies for the classes my kids were attending. The birthday*
> *parties were fun for me, as was trading baby-sitting chores*
> *with the neighbors for shopping trips and being a den mother*
> *for the Scouts.*
>
> —RITA

> *My twelve-year-old daughter is happy and moody, a friend*
> *who's fun to be with—usually!*
>
> —ANDREA

I Just Want to Feel Loved.

Having children to satisfy a hunger to feel loved can be an unhealthy motivation. This pitfall is common among intentional teen moms who see a child as the one person in the world who can't leave them and will always accept them.

> *I knew at fourteen or fifteen that if I had kids, everything would be OK. I could get away from all the bad stuff. It was an escape. I realize now that if I hadn't done that, I could've gone to college and been a professional.*
>
> —GINNIE

Once you are in your twenties and thirties, your motivations mature but may remain essentially the same at their root. Some women haven't found, or don't crave, an adult relationship and only desire the love of a child. Some women who are in a disappointing marriage hope a child will give them the love they're missing. While it's true that children are loving, childhood is designed around adults giving to the child, not the other way around.

> *Be true to yourself. Check the purposes, check your reasons. Is this for you? What's it for? Who's it for? The worst thing we can ever do to a child is have that child meet our needs instead of have us meet the child's needs.*
>
> —GLORIA

> *I sincerely believe my mother has diagnosable narcissistic disorder—everything was about her. I'm surprised that I'm*

*such a good mother. I found that instinctively I'm able to put
my daughter first.*

—PATSY

*If you're going to have a child to have someone love you, please
think twice. Young children are by nature highly egocentric,
and they come first.*

—FRAN

I Can Create a Being in My Own Image... or Maybe Not.

Another common motivation for parenthood is the idea that you can raise a child in your own image, with your values. True, children often grow up in your religion, with the same traditions and the same core principles for facing life's challenges. But prospective parents should be aware of the rather common instance when a child rebels against her parents, not just in adolescence, but also into adulthood. Liberal parents may suddenly realize they've raised a conservative child or a religious fundamentalist. Working-class parents who scrimped to send their child to college may find he comes back home with completely different values. Or well-heeled, conservative parents end up with a political rebel who gets arrested at nuclear plants or attacks whaling boats with dinghies.

> *There was a lot of pressure in my family to appear normal—to be like everyone else, to sit like a girl, dress like a girl, play like a girl. I would often get in trouble for being too rambunctious or too loud, or not sitting right or walking right, at church especially. We belonged to a very conservative church. I'm in a polyamorous relationship now. I've been married for eleven years, and I have a lover of five years who lives with us. We've decided not to have children.*
>
> —LARISSA

> *I came from a traditional family. My parents are conservative Jews, Holocaust survivors. They had a pretty old-fashioned*

view of what a family is. Being Jewish was a big part of
growing up, and part of that is having kids, being married. It
was just the expectation. So they've really had to adjust to my
choice to use a sperm donor and be a single mother by choice.

—ABBIE

What if I do everything I can, to the best of my ability, and this
kid still turns out to be a rotten person? Then what?

—WHITNEY

Then there are those of us who feel that with the right parenting, we could have turned out so much better, so we're motivated to have kids to correct the wrongs we feel were done by our parents. But no matter what we do, children are going to share some of our faults plus add a few they come up with on their own. A healthy sense of resignation will let you relax at times when your children are becoming the people they were meant to be, whether you like them or not!

My youngest son just turned eighteen. This is when you
want them to develop opinions and morals and hopefully
somewhere in there become an adult who's going to be sensi-
tive to others and caring. With men, have respect for women,
and for women, have respect for yourself. And for God's sake,
get an education, make some money, and take care of your
mother!

—PATTIE

As well as showing us new inner reserves of strength, imagination, patience, and happiness, raising children has a way of magnifying every weakness we've ever seen in ourselves. If you have ever felt inadequate to perform a chore like fixing the toilet, you can count on your child, at some point in his life, making you feel a thousand times more inadequate. If you have ever thought yourself too heavy or too thin, too pretty or too plain, you can be sure your child will let you know exactly what she thinks. A good sense of humor can go a long way at times like those.

I asked my daughter when she was five, "What's the worst thing you've ever put in your mouth?" and she said it was my cooking. It's things like that you just can't replace.

—AMY

A sense of humor can also help when and if you break it to the family that you *won't* be passing on the family genes.

I think early on I said to Mom, "You're not going to have any grandchildren; you're going to have to settle for granddogs." She said, "Does that make me a grandbitch?"

—LILLIE

It's Part of My Faith.

For some, religion is one of the strongest motivations for having a child and often one of the most rewarding support networks once you have a child. Religion, for many, is the first community we know outside of family. Childhood routines often revolve around a once-a-week visit to a house of worship or a home-based ritual. So before we can even speak, we know the lit candles, the chanting and singing, or the kneeling and folded hands common in most Judeo-Christian traditions and Islam.

The people from your religious community may feel entitled, even obliged, to ask questions about your decision to have children. If you choose to be child-free, though, their questions can become a source of either support and friendship or of betrayal and alienation. As in the family dynamic, you will have heard those questions, and the appropriate answers, many years before it's your turn to answer them.

For women who are ambivalent about their desire to have children, religion can offer the solace of faith that God will make it right, that an all-knowing force will give you the strength. A strong tradition of faith and an active support network for when the baby arrives can make a big difference to a new mom.

> We lived in the same house in the same small town the entire time, so our circle of friends remained the same, the community remained the same. It was a very supportive community. We were in a very strong Catholic parish.
> —ANGELA

In trying times, many a mother has prayed for that strength and successfully kept herself from harming her children or running away.

I laugh now, but I'm afraid it's true. Children are God's way of ensuring that you have a prayerful life!

—CANDI

A life grounded in a religion also provides the predictability and comfort of religious tradition. Christmas comes at the same time every year, and Hanukkah just about at the same time. Masses, services, and meetings are run in a reliable order with familiar songs and procedures. Older generations experienced the same rites of initiation. This kind of solid religious culture can be compelling and comforting for a woman deciding to be a mother, though disheartening for those who wished they had become mothers but couldn't.

They say that every Jewish marriage is like dancing on Hitler's grave, with the assumption you're going to have kids. So in some ways I feel like I've let my culture down by not having kids. A lot of Jews who marry Jews don't give their kids a Jewish upbringing, but I would have. Now the best I can hope to do is influence other people's kids.

—NORA

If your religious community does not support you, you can only look inside yourself if you know you will be acting against the official teachings of your faith.

I had a very good friend who had three children out of five who had muscular dystrophy. She went to the priest and said, "Can I please go on the pill?" He said, "No. It's God's will." One of the good women of the parish organized a prayer service for her, and my friend said, "What the hell is the matter with you? My kids are dying, and you want me to go to church and pray?"

—GINA

I'd Do It for Love.

A child is often the culmination of the expression of love between two people. For some couples, it's a no-brainer. They both want children, and they have them. But for women who struggle with the motherhood decision, deciding to live out the consequences of that particular expression of love is more complicated.

Having a child gives a couple a new experience together. Sometimes it seems like the next obvious step after marriage. Sometimes, once they've mastered the married-couple routine, they're looking for new challenges. And sometimes they decide that having a child would guarantee they would have something amazing, creative, fascinating, and exciting to work on together for the rest of their lives.

> *This is something we always planned for. It can do nothing but*
> *make our marriage stronger. It's something we want to*
> *enhance the relationship, a new way to spend time together.*
>
> —CHRIS

But there can be drawbacks to the strong love of one partner combined with the other partner's desire for children. It comes in the form of a woman who says, "If I truly love him, I'll give him a child if he wants one." She could just as well ask, "If he truly loves me, why would he want me to bear a child I don't want?" but she often doesn't.

If you decide to have a child against your own wishes or in the midst of overpowering ambivalence, you may be setting yourself up for a very difficult time. Although some ambivalent women become wonderful, well-adapted moms, others remain unhappy and risk causing confusion and unhappiness for their child. But if you're doing it for your partner's sake, then it's a double whammy, because you could be putting the entire relationship up for grabs.

But isn't that what love is? Giving, unconditionally? Yes . . . and no. A baby is "the gift that keeps you giving," to paraphrase a familiar jingle. It's not as though your partner will raise the baby alone or that you won't feel attached to or responsible for your child. You will always be the mom. But if you decide you want a child for your own reasons, on your own terms, you will bring a child into a much more stable and healthy family.

> *What does "doing it for him" really do for you, anyway? Let's be honest: it lets you off the hook. When the kid is too much to take, the first thing you'll say is, "You wanted this child." No kid should ever hear that, and no mother should ever think it.*
>
> *—KAREN*

> *We always give up things for other people, but if having a child is your strongest need, your strongest desire, will you be happy if you don't? Will you be able to look back through your childbearing years and say through it all, "I was happy"?*
>
> *—MELODY*

> *I'm not the kind of woman to get talked into things, but there I was, pregnant, wanting the baby, but not so sure I wanted to be a mom. He had told me that some day I'd want a child. I talked myself into it. But in the end, I had to face the truth; I did it for him and for the sake of the marriage, and I knew those were two lousy reasons.*
>
> *—DARCEY*

I'd Like to Build a Better World.

As children grow older, they begin to ask fascinating questions like, "Where do poor people come from?" and "What's war?" These questions often require parents to simplify very complicated issues, bringing your own views into sharper focus. They may motivate you to get involved in your community in ways you never have before and probably never would have except in response to your children.

Would you like to spend your days teaching children about the world? Are you excited about the idea of spending a holiday at a soup kitchen or a summer day at a community garage sale to raise money for the local crisis center? Does it sound like fun to take your children to art and natural history museums to open their minds to creative ideas or history?

> *All I truly hoped for was for them to be people who are conscious of other people, who can make a decent living and find some joy in their life. Hopefully, that's the kind of kids who will be citizens of the world, conscious citizens, conscious of color, of money, of the fact that material things don't count, but what's in your heart is what counts.*
>
> —JODI

> *We built a park together, and we did a weeklong barn raising. Even though my husband was much older, he taught them to sail. They were water babies.*
>
> —KARI

We had just moved into an apartment next to a bridge and some train tracks. My daughter was exploring. She came back to tell me that people lived under the bridge; she had seen their cardboard boxes and clothes. She said, "Let's take them some sandwiches." I was so pleased. She'd remembered the year before when we'd given sandwiches to a homeless man who had helped us get our kite out of a tree.

—LIZ

There are ways to have similar impacts on children without having your own. Many child-free couples take the children of their friends for a Saturday outing to give the parents a break. Women without children may volunteer at local women's shelters or work at day-care centers, exposing children to new ideas, answering their questions, and enjoying their company without having to take them home every night. There is more than one way to build a better world.

I've served as Guardian for a Job's Daughters Bethel (a fraternal organization for teenage girls) and as a teenage Sunday school teacher, with my husband. The kids loved us and told their families they got a lot out of what we were doing with them and teaching them.

—JO

2

Age Matters

The particular time in your life when you decide to have children or con-
clude you will never have children affects what your life will look like
long after you settle on your decision. Proper timing of motherhood can
enhance your mothering experience and your life in ways you could never
anticipate as you glide into a relatively uncomplicated, if challenging, new
lifestyle. Bad timing can let fate hit you broadside when pregnancy either
becomes more difficult than you expected or shows up long after you
thought it could. As you consider this decision, it helps to weigh the
social, financial, and emotional aspects of each stage of your life that will
make or break, support or discourage your choice.

Will There Be Other Moms My Age?

If you have children in your late teens or early twenties, most of your peers will still be single and likely to be getting their education, socializing at night, or establishing themselves in their first jobs. Though the community of moms of this age isn't large, it does exist. These women may be enjoying the early years of their young marriages or trying to make it as single moms. In either case, they're likely to be eager to find others in the same boat.

> *None of my friends wanted to hear about how lousy I felt being pregnant. They were talking about who was taking them to the prom. But the school had a teen mothers group, and I found a lot of help there.*
>
> —JESSE

From their midtwenties to midthirties are when most women have children or decide not to have children. As a mother, you will be a member of a substantial peer group of women with children, allowing you a broad range of women to talk to and share with.

Still, you face a varied and complex array of challenges. Having a child may seem like just another piece of your life puzzle or like yet another water balloon to keep in the air as you juggle other demands. But even an unplanned or mistimed pregnancy will be less disturbing to you and your partner at this age than an unplanned pregnancy would be for a very young or much older woman.

I find that most of the friends I see on a regular basis are friendships that have formed after I had kids. They are other women with children—neighbors, mothers of other kids on the team, classmates, and parents. These are the people I see all the time now. We have so much more in common.

—SANDRA

If you decide to have or adopt children when you're in your forties and fifties, expect to be an anomaly among your friends, since most of their children will be grown. They may be gladly on the other side of the adventure, and many will be in no rush to entertain little ones. On the other hand, your friends can become a deep well of parenting wisdom and experience when you most need to draw on it. You will likely find new friends of all ages in the parents of other children, and you'll have plenty in common when it comes to talking about your children. Inevitably, though, you'll have to face the question "Are you the grand-mother?" If you're happy with your decision and comfortable with your-self, you'll be able to shrug off such gaffes with a chuckle.

I felt completely out of step with the other generation—the parents of Tracy's friends. At the very beginning, like in a toddlers' tumbling class, the average age was twenty or eighteen. I kind of felt like a fraud, pretending to be the mother. I could easily be the grandmother. I didn't have a whole lot to talk about. I felt in the spotlight. It's not a problem now, but it was in the beginning.

—ELLA

I was disappointed with the reaction of some friends my age who had grown kids and had forgotten what it was like to have a toddler around. They treated us both with impatience and made me feel completely incompetent and inadequate as a mother.

—VICTORIA

Where Will I Be in My Career?

During the time you are in your midtwenties to midthirties, you are launching your career and professional life. You have invested time, energy, and resources in a trade or in higher education. Perhaps you're settling into one of your first "real" jobs, hoping to see a few promotions come your way.

This time in your life may be very focused on that career and what it has to offer, leaving little time for other pursuits, including children. On the other hand, if you've worked into your early thirties to develop your skills and contacts, you have the added benefit of a broader range of choices. A growing number of women are also discovering that being stay-at-home mothers and working at home are not only viable options, but attractive alternatives to the work world.

> *I'm not really tied to the whole idea of being a professor that much. Most people my age are still in grad school, so it would be fine if I needed to take time off and go back to it later.*
>
> —SHANA

> *I have drifted from job to job, trying to be a stay-at-home mom in between. I think after [my children] are all in school, I will go back to school so I can get a real job. I mean one that pays enough to pay for a sitter!*
>
> —STACY

By the time you reach your forties, you will likely be established in your career. You're comfortable. You have a pretty clear path in front of you and have had plenty of time to determine how having a baby affects that path. Compared with a younger woman, you may be more assertive about what you want out of your employer, because you have proven your worth and will have gained self-confidence. For the same reasons, you will also have gained a certain amount of bargaining power, and you'll be more willing to use it.

> *I've been with the company a number of years; I've proven myself. I've established myself. They're giving me this flexibility because I do a really good job and they value me. They realize I wouldn't be here if it weren't for that flexibility.*
>
> —MAGGIE

> *I arranged to work from home, on the computer, and to limit my responsibilities for the first six months after my son's birth.*
>
> —CHRISTINE

How Well Will I Know Myself?

Your personal development is still on the rise as you grow into your late twenties and early thirties. Many women are just getting comfortable with themselves at this age, just learning how to define themselves as they enter into a long-term love relationship. If you're still at the early stages of developing a strong sense of yourself, having a child now may impede that process. The abundance of Oprah-style talk shows focusing on women who have lost "their spirit" is one indication that this is a relatively common phenomenon.

> *When my children were very young and very needy, I was*
> *willing to be fairly passive in many of the decisions of our*
> *marriage. My energies were depleted for the common good.*
> *Now I am finding my voice again and sharing my input. At*
> *times it is difficult for my husband to negotiate with the newer*
> *me. So be it. I can't go back now.*
>
> —ADRIANNA

The women we talked to repeatedly emphasized that women who are still learning who they are and what they are capable of should wait to have children. It's a delicate balance between waiting and waiting too long, but it can result in a wonderful payoff of a stable, steady relationship and a happier life. Of course, since we never stop growing and developing, there are some things you just can't learn until you get there.

> *I have a clearer idea of what my limits are. I had never come up*
> *against them in so clear-cut a way before. I don't think you*
> *ever really know yourself until you've had your sleep destroyed*

and your temper provoked and your tenderness invoked the
way a small child can do.

—MARIA

One of the fortunate things about most women in their forties and fifties is that you usually know what you want. You've pursued just about every interest you've ever had, and experienced the advantages and short-comings of each one. A woman who wants a child at this age is determined to get one and generally thinks she knows what she's getting into.

By this time in your life, you have likely lived in at least one long-term relationship. You have learned many things about yourself and the people you love. You are often secure in who you are and can brush off the criticism and judgment that you took so seriously a few decades earlier.

I delivered at age forty. There weren't a lot of surprises in those
first few years. It's kind of like growing old. It's not like you go
from eighteen and gorgeous to seventy-five and wrinkled all in
one day or year. It's a gradual process, and the daily, weekly,
monthly, and yearly changes in the child aren't all that
noticeable. It just seems a natural transition from stage to
stage.

—LAURA

Will My Parents Be Around to Help?

Parents of women who choose to become mothers in their twenties and thirties are likely to be healthy and available to support the new parents, especially if the grandparents-to-be are moving into retirement and if they live close by or can travel. Since women during these years are often working, they may look to their parents for baby-sitting, advice, and moral support. This can be a proud and exciting time for grandparents eager to show off their grandchildren and their new family status, while their involvement gives new parents much-needed breaks.

We could be here another year or five or ten years. My parents are close by, and my mom's let it be known she's not averse to coming up and baby-sitting.

—LAVITA

I left a career in New York, where I worked for many years. Moving here was tough, but I did it to be closer to family. My parents have been great support.

—SARA

My daughter was colicky for five months. I remember waking up saying, "I just don't think I can do this anymore." We didn't have parents who live in this town; we couldn't say, "Here, take this child," and know she'd be treated well.

—DEDE

Older women having children often become a sandwich generation, caring not only for their children but for their elderly parents. So while you're adjusting to a new life with diaper bags and bottles, you may also be making crucial decisions about the health and well-being of your aging parents. Because of their advanced ages, you probably won't get much assistance in the baby-sitting department.

Right after my son was born, my mother-in-law's health went down. She couldn't live by herself anymore. My mother is a nurse—an amazing woman—who works at a nursing home. She suggested we put my mother-in-law in her nursing home, and it all worked out. But it was just a week after we moved into the new house with the baby that all this happened.

—MAGGIE

I've been through years of heavy responsibility caring for my parents. But they always took precedence, the parents, over my own needs and even my relationship. Now that I have a daughter, it's her turn. I can't do it all.

—JADE

How Will It Go with My Mother?

A move into motherhood in your twenties and early thirties may offer certain challenges in your relationship with your mother. You will almost inevitably begin to experience any unresolved tensions between you and your own mother. This can be an opportunity to improve and deepen your relationship, or it can be a chronic irritation that causes regular battles, depending on how you both decide to approach it.

> *If I can be a good mom, I won't be totally flawed. I think I felt totally flawed as a daughter—totally—smelly, ugly, fat, unpopular, unpretty, ungraceful, wrong.*
>
> —LINDSY

> *The fact that I didn't have Ward and June Cleaver parents didn't mean I couldn't have children and be happy and be a good person. My mom is my best friend now.*
>
> —VALERIE

A well-developed sense of your self and a commitment to resolve the issues with your mother can make your relationship much more enjoyable and helpful during this stressful time.

> *Both of my moms have always been there for me through my struggles with my daughter's illnesses. My stepmom raised me since I was three. My mom left because she liked the partying.*

Later she came back into my life. She and her boyfriend used to do drugs all the time, but she became born again. I just called her the other day and told her I could use a prayer.

—CYNTHIA

As you grow older, you get more opportunities to resolve issues with your mother, even if you haven't had children of your own. Many women find the strength to take advantage of those opportunities as they arise, and they put old, simmering resentments to rest. Sometimes the impending death of a parent can cause women to want children for the first time in their lives.

My father was diagnosed with cancer. My sister had adopted because she was infertile, and my brother is gay. I was between jobs and I had a good man, so I decided to have a baby. Looking back, I know my dad getting sick had something to do with why I had a baby when I did. I wanted him to know the family line would continue.

—CARRIE

Will I Find the Right Partner?

Women in their twenties and early thirties are often looking for a life mate to fill out the vision of their lives, but these days they are waiting longer to make lifetime commitments. As you wait to find a mate, you obviously limit the window in which you can decide to have children, unless you're willing to pursue single motherhood through artificial insemination or other arrangements. And yes, your fertility begins to drop at age twenty-seven, and then drops exponentially after your midthirties. This is one factor to consider when deciding about children, life mates, and alternatives, but it is certainly not the only one.

Waiting to find a partner can be a good thing if you are ambivalent about children. It may take a few years, some rough times, and some successes in other parts of your life to better help you assess whether or not you want children. Eventually, you'll want to find a partner who is on the same wavelength as you are about children. Your partner also plays a role in the best timing for a child. If your partner wants to pursue an advanced degree or has a promising but demanding career, then you may be left alone to raise your child much of the time. If your career stagnates, how will you feel about your partner's success and freedom from that schedule?

> *I was resentful that he decided to work six days a week for the next decade rather than be there for us. He felt that providing for his family was really his only and most important job. We benefited financially but lost big-time in the emotional, bonding, time-together, and sharing-the-experience kinds of ways.*
>
> —ELLEN

*He's always going to be working because he has the potential
to be making a lot more money than I could. I'll take the time
off.*

—SHIRLEY

An older partner's desire to have children or not will likely be clearer. A relationship in your later years is likely to be more stable because of your ages and your previous experiences. If you choose to become parents, your relationship will probably be able to withstand the trials and tribulations of parenthood with more flexibility and patience.

*We've been together a long time. We thought and talked about
the need to feel we were a family, so we adopted, and we're
both on board with it. We live in a balanced relationship.
Nobody's keeping a record, but one just fills in what the other
can't. It hasn't been the strain on our marriage I've seen in
younger couples.*

—MARILYN

Will I Have the Energy for Kids?

Women in their twenties to midthirties are generally able to maintain the energy level they need to chase around a toddler. They are also more likely than teen moms to have a supportive partner who will share in the childrearing.

Unlike your older counterparts, you'll probably still be active and healthy enough after your children are grown to enjoy life "after children" to its fullest. You may decide to renew vows with your partner, travel, or find other friends and interests. You will also be able to visit your own grown children and be active participants in their adult lives.

Energy becomes an issue in our later years. It's as if it drains out of us steadily from the day we're born, but we don't notice it until we try to do something we used to do in a blink of an eye twenty years earlier. Having and raising kids will bring out the reality of that lower energy supply immediately and in ways you may never before have imagined.

> With all the advice that came to me from good friends my age, it wasn't until I became Emily's mother I realized I hadn't a clue. When they told me, "You won't have time to do music, et cetera," I just discounted it. I'd always had pressures, and I'd handled it. It was a serious adjustment and took a tremendous amount of energy. That first one was an emotional year, a stressful year for everybody.
>
> —JOYCE

Regular exercise and overall good health can go a long way toward maintaining higher energy levels, but if you decide to become a mom at a later age, sleep deprivation, backaches, and overall exhaustion will be magnified for you, thanks to that extra decade or two. Then, as if that weren't enough, as your children are reaching adolescence, you could be reaching menopause, two hormone-laden stages clashing in one household.

As your children are about to go off to college, you'll be facing retirement or be well into it. Energy and health could play a role in how interested you'll be in visiting them at college or baby-sitting for the grandkids. And as one older mother pointed out somberly, there is a good chance she won't be around to enjoy that part of her daughter's life.

What About Stability?

Younger couples are often going through many changes—in their educations, careers, or as we mentioned earlier, personal development.

Couples in this age bracket are working hard to move up in the world, build their nest egg, and create some sense of financial security for the future. These couples generally have the skills and education to provide good opportunities for their children and to set aside some funds for college. To do this, though, many couples at this stage are socking away those savings, which means budgeting carefully and saying no to things their child-free counterparts can purchase without hesitation.

If you end up having children and then raising them on your own, you may be able to successfully redesign your life around single motherhood. Even so, you will likely be hoping for some good fortune to go along with your hard work.

> *After my husband died, it was pretty challenging to know I had to do all the work with the kids. We had one income, and there wasn't very much insurance. It was scary. I had the terrible nightmares of taking a test and I didn't get to practice. "I'm not taking the test." "You have to." "What if I don't?" "Your children will die." It was a repeating dream. It's scary to be completely responsible without a safety net. But I ran my business out of my home, and they learned they had to be quiet when the phone rang.*
>
> —RACHEL

Older women and their partners are likely to be established in a career. They probably have already purchased a home and furnishings—and paid for them. They have likely set aside considerable retirement savings and are living comfortably. An older mother also has the wisdom of her years. You might be just as inept at changing a diaper as any first-time mother, but you have learned patience, how bad and good things never last, the depth and strength of love, the illusion of infatuation, and you have experienced pain and loss and joy. If you can maintain your energy and live a long, healthy life, you will be able to pass on this wisdom in a way most younger mothers cannot.

> *I work with child protection, and my coworkers were guffawing that after sixteen years of marriage, we finally had kids. "Now do you understand why people abuse their kids?" they'd say. I said to their faces that now I have less tolerance than ever for people who abuse their kids.*
>
> —DARYL

3

Why Am I Worried?

Let's be honest: it's scary to think of having and raising children. We are concerned that we're not up to the task, that we'll become overwhelmed, that we will raise someone who will resent us, or that we can never live up to what our parents achieved. But women are no strangers to fear. We walk confidently down city streets past groups of men, take the train home late at night, stand up to our managers, find a lump in our breasts.

Other women often support us in facing these fears and concerns. Will they support us through our ambivalence over motherhood? We don't know.

We worry that we're being less womanly to admit any fear or doubt about what many consider our most basic instinct and our most important social role: to be a mother. Yet keeping these concerns silent does not help us address them.

Will I Lose Myself?

It is true that once you decide to have children, life as you know it will never be the same. Usually, when a woman talks about "losing herself," she means losing control over her life. When you get pregnant and have a child, you have to give up, at least temporarily, control over your time, your body, in fact, almost everything. It's normal, but it often blindsides new mothers. This can be very disconcerting to some women.

> *Having a child affected my career* majorly! *I was in management. I had a great job, great paycheck, great stock options. But I got so sick after my daughter was born, and she was born so early, I just couldn't bear to leave her to return to work.*
>
> —LISA

> *Everything takes twice as long as you expect it to!*
>
> —MONA

Having a child inevitably means losing some control to do what you want when you want. Children get sick and need attention, day care falls through, and children want to spend time with their parents—often when it's not convenient. But having children does not have to mean losing control over everything in your life nor losing the person you have become. The question to ponder is how much control you are willing to give up and for how long.

Can I "Do It All"?

For all the rewarding moments when your baby giggles, your toddler blurts out an amazing question, or your teenager shows good judgment, there will be other times when you will grieve some of the trade-offs you've made to become a mom. It's only natural to long for your old lifestyle with its Saturday nights out, hobbies, reading time, or workouts.

Having a child means adding a second shift to your current workday, and more and more women are appreciating how difficult and undesirable it can be to try to work a lifetime of second shifts. They either give up much of what they did before they became mothers or decide that motherhood isn't worth what they know they'd have to give up. As you think about how you spend your time now, consider what it would be like to have a baby or toddler in tow as you try to do what you most enjoy. Will it be possible? Will it be worthwhile to give up some of that? How much would you regret what you left behind? Are there realistic ways you can see including enough of those things in a life with children to keep you happy and fulfilled?

> *Little ones want your attention all the time. There is little time for you. One thing I did was train my children that every day they would have to give me time to myself—one hour. They were OK with that.*
>
> —SHANNON

> *As the years went by and I had more children, I could better anticipate some of our needs and begin to lay the framework of*

appropriate support. Lots of watching videos so I could rest.
Household help three hours a week.

—HANH

The one thing that women who "do it all" usually cannot do is take time for themselves. Given the challenge of motherhood, that's no surprise.

I was really close to having it all, but when I was almost there,
I had nothing. I ended up hating it all. I thought that once I
had it all, people would walk up to me on the street and say,
"I hear you have it all; how great!" You get no brownie points
for doing it all, and you're constantly coming up short in all of
your departments—work, husband, child, yourself, and all the
things that take a lot of time that no one talks about like the
eighteen thank-you notes that have to get written or calling
shoe stores because we went to two of them Saturday to find
out they didn't stock ballet flats.

—GEORGENE

If you are a totally independent career-woman, social-climber
type, consider not having children. If you are thirteen to
twenty-five and don't want to be bothered with the total
responsibility of caring for another human being for at least
the next twelve years, including cleaning, feeding, diapering,
cleaning up vomit and feces, not sleeping for nights on end,
having absolutely no social life, I beg you, don't have children!
You'll be glad!

—FRANCES

Can I Handle the Responsibility?

Some women who previously focused primarily on their own needs take on an entirely new perspective when they get pregnant and decide to become a mother. Family and friends can be amazed by your sudden desire to protect your health and your baby's health from harmful outside forces. Before your baby was born, you may have had a hard time getting home before midnight. After the baby, you may suddenly become a "nester," perfectly content to stay at home and coo over your baby. This can be a time of incredible growth and an opportunity to learn new things about your own inner strength and abilities.

I have grown along with my children, acknowledged when I am wrong (and they are right), and feel confident I am a better person because of them.

—HANNAH

I think my children made me saner. Less self-involved equals saner in my book. They also make me happy. Happy is good.

—STEPHANIE

My first child helped motivate me to make huge changes in my life. At the time I became pregnant, I was very unsettled, prone to making decisions on a whim and without a lot of thought to

the consequences. Becoming a parent made me much more
responsible.

—SIMONE

But a routine that suddenly means not going out in the evenings because the baby has to get to bed can feel like a noose around the neck to some women. How important is it to you to be free to pick up and go for a drink if a friend calls at 9:00 P.M.? How will you feel the morning you wake up with the flu and you're the only one home to comfort and care for your crying, wet, hungry baby?

In recent years I've been diagnosed with an autoimmune
condition, but I've always been tired. When others were down
for a day with a cold, I was down for a week. There's no way I
could take care of another human being in that condition.

—HELEN

I do like my independence, doing whatever I want to when I
want to, and not being responsible for anyone but me. I can
barely get me together some days; I don't know how anybody
does it with kids.

—JORDAN

Will I Like My Child? Will My Child Like Me?

You'd be surprised. Children are amazingly resilient and accepting, and becoming a parent has a strange way of making adults that way as well. Still, plenty of people have heard the two-year-old tantrum in the grocery store—"I *hate* you!"—and maybe, in the back of their minds, have wondered how the mom feels at that moment as well.

> When my sister-in-law had a baby, we went to see her. In the hospital room she was in a lot of pain and wasn't anywhere near the baby. I thought, "Oh, my God, what if I don't like the baby?" What's scaring me is that I can't bond with it while I'm pregnant, and I feel like I should. The whole dream that I have is that after my birth, I'm going to be sitting up in the hospital bed holding the baby, not thinking about the pain, waiting for people to come visit. But that's not what my sister was doing at all.
>
> —MEGAN

Most expectant moms aren't ready to hear about this until after they've delivered. Then the doubts set in. A young mother in the hospital bed wonders why her baby doesn't respond to her, but newborns don't respond to *anyone*. Mothers of toddlers wonder if their children really mean it when they say they "hate" them. During every stage of your child's development, at one time or another, you are likely to worry about whether your child likes you.

I honestly thought it would get easier as they got older. The demands are still there, just different. I rejoiced in his increasing independence, but sometimes it really made me sad as well. Sometimes when he doesn't need me, it feels like he doesn't like me.

—ANNETTE

Sometimes I am just overcome with a feeling, much like the first time you fall in love with someone. All this is much more overpowering than I had expected.

—TONI

The concern about your relationship with your children never goes away, and a lot of struggles with toddlers seem to come back in very similar ways a decade later with adolescence.

We had two kids in Catholic high school and one in Catholic grade school. The two older ones were angry with me when their father left. How were they going to get a car? The source of their money was gone. This was my fault. The best part is that my daughters came to respect me . . . and after a lot of grief, a lot of therapy, every one of them knows she can do it alone. That's another thing I credit myself with—they can think for themselves. They can think.

—ANGELA

Young people will test your confidence, make you question your decisions, and cause you to feel like an amateur at just about everything.

You need to be smart and brave. On days when you can't be smart and brave, you need to be able to laugh about it. Babies don't know that their shirt is dirty, but they know if you're happy to see them.

—NICOLLET

Will I Become My Mother?

Some women want to do whatever they can to avoid becoming their mothers. Others wonder if they could ever live up to the exalted example their mothers set. Becoming a mother is like much of our other learning: we hope to copy characteristics from those around us whom we admire, and we try to avoid characteristics we don't like. Unfortunately, we don't always succeed on either or both fronts.

> *I had this tremendous frustration of what had gone awry with me as a child, then this overwhelming feeling of the need to fix it—to control it and fix it. I'm terrified if I don't remain hypervigilant, I'm going to slip up and become my mother.*
> —RHIANNA

> *The way our parents raised us is how we want to raise our children. It's very much old school. I just want to relive my childhood with my child. My mother was crabby, generous, and traditional. We have a good relationship now, but growing up, we never clicked. Once I got to college, it was OK.*
> —MARY ANNE

Becoming a mother allows you to understand the woman you've always known as "Mom" from a different perspective. If you decide to become a mother, you will almost inevitably hear yourself saying the very things you swore as a child that you would never say to *your* kid. There may be times you even *do* things you swore you would never do to your kid. These words and deeds run the gamut from the old standby of "because I said so" to much more harmful physical and emotional abuse.

As you find yourself echoing some of your mother's traits, your response can vary from forgiving to vigilant. Identifying those traits and recognizing their impact can go a long way toward managing your fear. For instance, minor infractions such as "because I said so" or making your child bundle in multiple, stuffed layers before going out to play in the snow give you the opportunity to look back at the woman your mother was, accept her, and even laugh at how life comes full circle. More hurtful behavior is a sign that you may need to get help. The problem may be more than you can handle alone, but it's one that can be handled if you call in reinforcements.

> I was in therapy, trying to be a mother, and I was figuring out my relationship with my mother. That's what happens when you have a child, because you both understand your mother and are frustrated with her. You want to demand, "Why weren't you this or that kind of mother?"
>
> —MINDY

> I don't put my daughter on the spot; I do not ever embarrass her in front of other adults, and I hope to God I never do. My mother embarrassed me all the time.
>
> —RAE

What if I Really Don't Want Children?

Women are bombarded from their earliest childhoods with the notion that they will become mothers. We end up with little voices inside of us telling us we aren't complete women, our partners won't love us, or our parents will be so disappointed if we don't have children. Women who are child-free by choice must quiet those voices and move on.

When I was in high school, I just assumed I would grow up, get married, and raise Presbyterian children. That was just the expectation of girls at the time. It's a really good thing I didn't have children, because they'd just be in the way. I never really had the urge to be a mother. I never really thought I'd love to have little lives to mold, noses to wipe, nursery rhymes to read.

—BETTY

I just assumed that we would have kids. But he brought it up early in our relationship that he did not want children. Truthfully, between my work and taking care of children, plus myself, there'd be no time for myself in that mix. I love my job, I really do. I would not want to give that up. There's really no way I can see making work a part-time thing that would be gratifying to me professionally.

—LEANN

If you find yourself feeling pressured to have children and almost deciding to have children "by default," you may want to take another look and examine what is motivating you. In the end, you will be their mother, and you will be responsible for them for the rest of your life. Long after your parents are gone, and possibly your spouse, you will most likely be the one raising your child. Make sure the decision to be a mother was one you made for yourself. (We will discuss this more in Chapter 6, "What Does Having Children Do to a Relationship?")

Am I Selfish if I Don't Have Children?

Women who make the nontraditional decision to be child-free often face surprise and alarm when friends and family learn that children aren't on the horizon. You may not be able to change what other people think, but remember, the choice is yours.

The women we spoke to who had decided not to have children were honest and comfortable with their decision. Some acknowledged that they *were* being selfish—in response to this unspoken charge against them—but redefined the word: being selfish, they said, means taking care of one's self and recognizing it means never giving your child short shrift. Others pointed out that the assumption that a childless woman was a selfish woman is tied to the old idea that childbearing is every woman's duty. And still another woman suggested that selfishness can exist on both sides of the choice; for example, some people who have children are selfishly seeking the unconditional love a young child promises.

Women who choose not to have children report the feeling of freedom that the decision has given them in every aspect of their daily lives and in planning their futures. They say they have more options, and they have more time to devote to their careers and their relationship with their partner.

I look at my sister, and she has more or less put her life on hold to raise her three children. Her outside interests have had to

*dwindle. Without children, my own life didn't go on hold
because I had to run this child here or that child there.*

—JEANNE

Women who have chosen not to have children often have developed a standard response to people who either ask why or rudely insist they should have children. Here are some of the most effective responses:

- "I (we) have thought a lot about it and decided having children isn't right for me (us). It's such a personal decision, you know."
- "We've decided not to have children. Tell me about your children."
- "We have dogs instead. They keep us plenty busy!"

One of these responses is usually enough to change the subject.

If I Don't Have Kids, Will I Feel Lonely When I'm Old?

Women who have decided not to have children are eager to point out that having them is no guarantee you won't be alone in your old age. True enough. There are abundant stories about children moving away from, ignoring, or neglecting their elderly parents, just as there are stories at the other end of that spectrum. Women without children have resolved to call upon friends and extended family for assistance—and will pass on heirlooms and other belongings to them as well.

> *Growing old alone is absolutely not a reason to have children. I still have a lot of family around me that are very loyal to me and wouldn't simply leave me somewhere by myself. I am a very social person. If I end up by myself in a nursing home situation, I will just make friends there.*
>
> —LEXI

Even women who have made the most resolute decision against having children are bound to feel a certain degree of loss or absence from time to time, especially if they spend time with children in happy, healthy settings. This feeling doesn't necessarily mean that they made the wrong decision, just as occasional regrets after having kids doesn't necessarily mean you shouldn't have had them. Life is full of gray. Each choice has some positives and some negatives.

We talk about this a lot after a weekend of baby-sitting my niece and nephew, who are two and four. I know how exhausted I am after that. It's a good reminder every once in a while.

—RHEA

Young relatives provide the kind of playful innocence many childless women might otherwise miss. Some childless women consciously go into professions that put them in the midst of children, such as pediatrics or elementary-school teaching. Still others become Big Sisters or unrelated "aunts" to the children of their friends. And then there are those who fill their lives with activities that feel playful—such as writing, art, sculpture, or acting. Many women also find a special added measure of love and companionship through pets.

When someone would say, "I would die for my children," I always thought that was a cop-out. Then two years ago, we got our first pet, and it has changed my life. The absolute love and devotion, no matter what, that this living creature gives me . . . these dogs of mine have created such a warmth and such a love.

—BECKA

Many pet lovers can attest to the intense bond they have with their pets. This is not to say that someone who has had a child and a pet would find the two comparable, but for women who have not experienced raising children, pets may bring them closest to an expression of the unconditional love mothers feel for their children.

The women we spoke to had thought long and hard about their decision not to have children. Some just did not have the opportunity. Some faced a long regimen of infertility treatments they could not tolerate or afford. Others simply concluded that their priorities did not include raising kids. No matter what the origins of their decision in favor of childlessness, all of these women warned against making the decision not to have children without careful consideration.

It was a decision that evolved over time—a combination of changing focus on what was important in my life. If the right person had come along in my twenties, I almost surely would have had children, and I think I would have regretted it deeply.

—BETH

We saw that the women who expressed the most regret were those who wanted the experience of raising a child but eventually realized it was too late in life. Those who had consciously decided not to have children occasionally had some regrets, of course, but on the whole were satisfied they had made the best decision for them.

4

What Will Pregnancy Do to My Health?

Many popular pregnancy books can walk you through what to expect when you become pregnant. Two of the bestsellers are *What to Expect When You're Expecting* and *Pregnancy for Dummies* (a scary title if we've ever heard one!), both of which can explain the day-to-day, week-to-week changes in your body.

There is plenty of time to learn about hormonal changes and episiotomies. For now, it's enough to highlight some of the physical and emotional joys, surprises, and challenges that lie ahead for women who decide to have children.

What if I'm Still Ambivalent After I Get Pregnant?

The ambivalence surrounding the decision to become a mother doesn't end with a positive pregnancy test. In fact, for some women, it's just the beginning. Your ambivalence will be strongly affected by whether the pregnancy is planned and whether the father is supportive. It is also a good sign that you are taking this decision very seriously and doing your best to plan ahead for your new life. Some of what you'll feel can also be attributed to the fluctuation in your hormones as your body adjusts to pregnancy.

On good days, you'll be on top of the world. You'll feel in love with your partner, if you have one, and in love with this being growing inside of you. You'll feel confident that you've got it all figured out and that, no matter what, you'll be a great mom.

On bad days, you'll wonder how you ever got into this mess. You'll try to figure out ways to undo it, go back and start over, or pretend it isn't happening. You'll feel like you have an alien growing inside of you and wonder why anyone would sign up for such duty. You'll look at your lover with suspicion and feel convinced that your boss is ready to fire you.

I went through donor insemination by myself. Then I bought this test, and that night I did it, and it came back positive. I was absolutely shocked. I didn't tell anyone. I waited till morning. I was very anxious and had to take some time off from work. I spent the next few days thinking about it. Was this what I wanted? When it doesn't work the first time and

*you don't get pregnant, you have that chance to feel
disappointed and think again about what you really wanted.
This was kind of a leap of faith.*

—SHERI

If you get no respite from your ambivalence, it may be time to consider terminating your pregnancy before it's too late. Abortion is an option within the first trimester. While you may never have considered abortion before, carefully examining what a lifetime of motherhood would mean for you may cause you to look into it more carefully. Women's health clinics that offer abortion services provide information about the procedure as well as your other options. For some women, it's the right decision.

*I was fifteen when I got pregnant. I just pretended I wasn't
pregnant. I would've had an abortion, but I was too
embarrassed to tell anyone. I just couldn't do it, not because
I didn't believe in abortion, but because I just couldn't do it.
I wish I'd had an abortion. I put her up for adoption. She's
twenty now. I can't be around her. She has a lot of problems,
I'm sure because of her low birth weight. She's been in a
mental facility from when she was little—lots of meds,
flashbacks, delusions. It's not that her life isn't worth
having . . . but still . . .*

—BARB

Is Childbirth as Rough as It Looks?

Childbirth is usually a painful process. But take comfort in knowing that modern medications and procedures can allow you to manage your pain and emerge from the childbirth experience with a sense of triumph or mastery. You and your health professional have a number of options, including childbirth classes, a variety of anesthetics, and other pain management techniques for making the best of childbirth.

In addition, there is some truth to the statement of so many women that childbirth is the most forgettable pain.

> *I was in labor for thirty-eight hours! Thankfully, I only had to push for the last three. It was exhausting. Yeah, I have to admit, there were times I thought evil thoughts about my husband, even as he stood there holding my hand. But once you're there, there's no going back. You just get through it the best you can and hope you don't make a fool of yourself. Drugs help!*
>
> —SUE

> *I didn't even know I was in labor. I came out of the bathroom and thought my bladder had fallen apart, so I went back in the bathroom and smelled my underwear because they say it smells different than urine. And my husband walked in and*

said, "What are you doing?" So he took me to the hospital, and the water kept coming out. I took a towel, wore sweatpants, but it was uncomfortable when it kept coming out and you're lying in it on the table.

—KAREN

In the end, only you can decide if the anticipation of a few hours of pain will be the deal-breaker in your decision to have children.

Is There Sex After Childbirth?

Many couples wonder whether they can expect a good sex life after they have children. The answer depends on who you ask. The mother of a newborn may look at you in horror at the suggestion, but give her another six weeks or a couple of months, and she'll be more interested. Nature has a way of making sure humans keep procreating, though women report different experiences of sex after having a baby. Breastfeeding may cause your vagina to be drier than normal, which your partner could mistake as a sign of disinterest. Or you may truly *lack* interest after having a baby hanging on you for what feels like the entire day.

> *We had much less sex. I was very tired at the end of the day and really most often just wanted to have some time to myself when I plopped into bed.*
>
> —ANNIE

> *Frankly, an intimate relationship was almost nonexistent while the children were growing up. I was terrified of getting pregnant again, and I felt consumed by the children.*
>
> —ELENA

The spontaneity is often gone because of the demands of the child or children. However, the planning that goes into paying attention to each other can often enhance the relationship. Successful, happy couples make time for each other—an important aspect of maintaining a healthy relationship after the baby is born.

> *I think children enhanced our romantic relationship. Sneaking sex when you share a hotel room is exciting. Being a mother makes me feel more like a woman. Pregnancy and childbirth unlocked a whole new world of femininity.*
>
> —LIZA

> *All children are born with "boner radar." Just try and get intimate with kids present. Yeah, even sleeping ones.*
>
> —ANNIE

> *As a single mother, my response was to just tune this aspect out of my life.*
>
> —PEG

Women also have a physical basis for their fear of sex after childbirth. Since women can't see all of our genitalia, we can't check if everything's OK. You may have an episiotomy (an incision between the vagina and anus that is made during childbirth) that is still healing, or you worry that your vagina has stretched and you won't be sexually appealing anymore. If you've had a cesarean section, you'll have a long line of fresh abdominal stitches.

> *Of course, there's wear and tear on the body. The expanded rib cage and hips. The episiotomies (four) and the healing of the scar. To top it all off, at the end of my fourth pregnancy, I had an undiagnosed kidney stone that was lodging and not passing for three months off and on.*
>
> —LETICIA

> *I had a tendency to lump all of my physical woes together and blame them on the pregnancy or the baby. I was older, more tired, and busier, and maybe just not taking care of myself. Later, it was easier to blame the kids than to say I should get some rest or go to the gym more often.*
>
> —TOBY

I'm Afraid to Say I'm Afraid.

Let us count the fears: labor, motherhood, relationship, job—the list goes on and on. It's normal to be afraid, but the best way to counter fear is with knowledge. The second best way is with confidence. If you know what you're getting into and you trust in your own strength, you can carry off just about anything, motherhood included.

Among the other fears and concerns we address in Chapters 3 and 11, many pregnant women also discover a fear of becoming a victim. They dream they will be attacked, or they have a heightened awareness of shady characters walking past them down the street. This may well be an instinctive response to protecting a fetus, but it can be very disconcerting to women who are usually confident about their ability to protect themselves in most situations.

> I never felt so vulnerable as when I was pregnant. I lived in a big city, where I was always nervous anyway. I couldn't run as fast if I needed to get away. I couldn't maneuver as well in general. And every man I walked by on the street seemed to be a threat. I knew it was irrational, but I couldn't stop myself.
>
> —DARLENE

Many pregnant women also fear that their present condition and future mother role will make them permanently unappealing to their partners.

> In the past couple weeks, I've been having dreams that my husband would be talking to other women, and I'd be so

jealous. I may be thinking I may not be sexy and I may not be what he wants anymore.

—TRACEY

There are plenty of times the fear will seem overwhelming and even end up targeting the people you love most, including your partner. For most women, these fears, like the ambivalence and occasional depression, are a temporary phenomenon.

What if I'm Not Happy Right Away?

Many pregnant women and new mothers feel like there is something wrong with them if they don't feel positive emotions as soon as they discover they're pregnant, or even in the first few weeks after the birth of their child. They worry that they are the only women in the world who have felt this way. They are not.

An unplanned pregnancy, the prospect of labor and then childbirth (whether or not the pregnancy was planned), and looming life changes can all contribute to a pregnant woman's anxiety, siphoning good feelings from the big news. A woman who experiences a completely joyous pregnancy may be shocked to discover an unresponsive newborn, but actually it'll be a few weeks before a mom sees the first smile from her child. When reality falls short of the high expectations a woman may have of motherhood, she can begin to doubt herself and wonder if something is wrong with her. But for almost every woman, this is only a passing phase.

> *When I found out I was pregnant, my first concern was whether or not I was going to lose my job. The next concern was finding affordable and adequate child care. Next was what I was going to do about having to take time off work to attend to the baby's needs. No matter how you cut it, corporate America is not kind to mothers.*
>
> —KAYLESHA

My first child and I did not truly bond until he was close to one year old. I was quite disillusioned because my perceptions were based on the idea that motherhood is all wonderful happiness and joy.

—YOLANDA

At two months, she was on the changing table, and I was talking to her, trying to ignore the horrible bowel movement, getting her all cleaned up fresh and dry, looking at her. All of a sudden, she coos back and she's smiling, and it's her first attempt to communicate. It was like nine months of pregnancy and two months of twenty-four-hour care finally paid off. That was so rewarding and so needed at that point. That really helped, this being recognizing me and reaching out to me.

—EMMA

New moms who experience almost no joy in the first few months may be slowly sliding into despair. The downward spiral—if left unchecked—can be devastating. You feel like you ought to be so happy at this time in your life, but you're not. Then you get angry at yourself for not being happy like any "good" mother would be, and that makes you feel even worse. Now more than ever, people are recognizing that the early stages of motherhood can be more than one woman can handle. A supportive partner and understanding friends and relatives can offer to help you if you need more time to adjust, by taking the baby and letting you know it's OK to get some time to yourself. Of course, if that isn't enough, a professional can help you learn new coping mechanisms for your new challenges.

I was so unhappy for the first eight or nine months. My husband gave me a negligee for a gift, and it was the first time I felt like I wasn't just a giant breast whose sole existence was for feeding my baby.

—TONI

Will I Lose My Shape Forever?

This depends largely on how important your shape is to you. If you are a woman who goes to the gym three days a week or always finds time to run a few miles a day, then it is likely that you *will* find the time and the way to get your shape back. You will need to accommodate the new demands of your life, including around-the-clock care for your newborn and the sleep deprivation that most women experience in the first few months. But the odd shape and form of your body immediately after childbirth can be amazing inspiration for overcoming these obstacles.

Vaginal childbirth does cause a necessary widening of the hips, or more accurately, pelvic bones, to allow the baby to pass through. But that widening isn't permanent, and you can gain back your original shape as the cartilage firms up.

Of course, there are more long-term effects of pregnancy on most women's bodies. Whether or not medical science bears it out, plenty of women report that it's much harder for them to lose weight and tone up after pregnancy. The flabby belly that pregnancy causes can be frustratingly difficult to get rid of, and stretch marks don't disappear on most women. It may be the new routine that leaves little time to exercise, the menu that is often determined by how much time you have to fix it and what the kids are willing to eat, or some combination of age and these new lifestyle changes that contribute to your new shape. In addition, your hair may thin out a bit, your bladder may not be what it used to be, and breastfeeding—for all its benefits to your baby—can cause your breasts to lose density and change their shape for good.

Well, I have stretch marks on my belly, and my bladder seems to be a little weaker, but I just don't wear a bikini (my boys

*would just say, "Gross, Mom," anyway), and I walk a little
faster to the bathroom.*

—CORINNE

*Before pregnancy, I was great at exercising, but after that,
something was gone with the motivation, energy, time to do
that. So I didn't exercise.*

—MELISSA

*I have migraines all the time now, and my hips don't want to
go back to my size six. This bothers me because we do not have
the money for me to go on a shopping spree to get larger
clothes.*

—MATTIE

While these changes can be distressing to some women, others learn
to accept them. Some women even wear them as a badge of motherhood.
Some women report an unexpected pleasure that comes with their new
motherly figure.

*I have made peace with my little bulge below the belly button—
and threw bikinis out the door!*

—LISA

*Pregnancy made my shape better. My husband enjoys my
"curves." The weight I put on is typical of pregnancy. I am
actually smaller in my waist now than I was before I had my
first daughter, and I am twenty pounds heavier.*

—MARY

*My partner says my breasts are more beautiful now than they
were when I was twenty-two. He always says he has my
daughters to thank for that.*

—NORMA

Will I Be Happy When It's Over?

The joy parents feel at the sight of their newborn baby is almost indescribable. Many women try to express the depth of the joy they experience in feeling the fetus kick for the first time, having their baby and holding it in their arms, or taking it home and learning to breastfeed it. There is no limit to the excitement and wonder parents feel as their baby becomes more responsive to them after the first few weeks. As their infant grows, it transfixes the adults around it with cute smiles, tiny arms reaching out, and silly cooings. Many women say their baby taught them more about love than any other life experience.

> I loved being pregnant. The experience of feeling the baby kick, the baby growing, seeing the baby's heartbeat on the ultrasound. Everyone used to laugh at me because I had a huge smorgasbord at my desk—I had permission to eat.
>
> —CARMEN

> I have felt joy for the first time in my life. I am calmer and more able to see things for what they are. I am more patient and nonjudgmental.
>
> —MARIA

But not all women are happy after the birth of their child. Instead, they are surprised by the lack of response they get from their newborn or overwhelmed by the reality of interrupted sleep, the smell and mess of diapers, and at times the overpowering sense of isolation.

My first baby cried so much. I had a lot of difficulties dealing with how to handle life at all. I was not prepared for that.
—LARISSA

I felt lonely because I had no "mom friends"—my mom friends all worked. I didn't have a neighborhood where I would see other women with strollers. I felt isolated that way. I didn't have any relatives nearby.
—ANDREA

Will I Get Depressed?

Many women go through pregnancy and postpartum never experiencing depression. But for women who have a tendency toward depression, pregnancy doesn't provide any protection against it. For many women, pregnancy is an exhilarating time, full of celebration, joy, and more positive attention than they've ever received before. For others, it can be the greatest challenge they ever face. Financial worries, an unplanned pregnancy, career interruption, troubles in the relationship, and even oppressively hot weather can wear a spirit down. Often, because it is so gradual and is considered forbidden during such a "happy" time, a woman doesn't realize or can't admit she's depressed. Her friends, family, and health professional must be able to read the signs.

> *Postpartum depression was horrible. I work with people who have depression, and it gave me insight into what they experience. I didn't recognize it at the time. I was crying over stuff in her baby book or who was going to return stuff to the library. It lasted probably just a few days, but I was afraid at the time because I didn't know how long it would last. Those first few months were very, very tiring. When I went back to work at eight weeks, it felt better, less tiring, than being at home all day with her.*
>
> —JULIA

Women with diagnosed mood disorders no longer have to choose between treatment and keeping their pregnancy safe. Historically, there has been a lot of concern about using antidepressants during pregnancy, although these medicines haven't been associated with fetal abnormalities. The current trend in treatment focuses on the possible impact that a mother's psychiatric condition could have on the health of her fetus or child. So if you have any history of mood disorders, talk to your psychiatrist and gynecologist before deciding to become pregnant—or as soon as you know you are pregnant, if you didn't discuss it earlier.

Will I feel out of Control?

If you like to be in control, pregnancy is your training ground for a new way of being for the rest of your life. It's time to let go a little. You can't control the kicking of the baby in the middle of the night, the hemorrhoids, the varicose veins, the heavy breasts, the backache, or the lack of sleep. You can't control the people who think your belly is community property once you become pregnant, or that the process itself takes forty weeks but sometimes feels like forty years. Impatience, common among pregnant women, is a sign of wanting that control and wanting it all to be done with. "Get on with having the baby already," you tell your body in the ninth month, but the baby comes when it feels like it and not a minute sooner. This is only the beginning of the adventure, a world unlike any other, where this other human being determines its own and your fate much of the time, and control is just an illusion!

> *You really want to do something when you're pumping other than looking at your breast. It's a real competitive thing—I'm looking at my breast and saying, "Faster, faster!" It's very frustrating.*
>
> —ALICE

> *Being a career woman, I'm a real multitasker. It was real hard for me to just sit down and enjoy my baby and nurse her and be in that moment. I felt like it's very time-consuming and that I should be getting more done. I was lucky if I took a shower those first few weeks. I've definitely adjusted—she's in control!*
>
> —MARTI

Are There Special Challenges for Lesbian Moms?

Lesbian couples that decide to have a baby will confront many of these emotions and then some. While coping with hormones and moods, as well as physical changes, you may also encounter a resistant medical establishment and less-than-supportive responses from your family and straight friends.

This is the time for you to be more assertive than ever about your needs and, if in a couple, more supportive than ever of each other. Interview your prenatal care provider before starting care to make sure he or she will be completely supportive. A sensitive provider will also alert the hospital staff about you and your partner's needs during labor and delivery. This is often a time when family support would feel wonderful, but if it isn't there, limit contact with family members who aren't helpful and happy for you.

> *Our hospital had a "husband pass" that lets husbands have access to the maternity ward anytime. At first, they didn't want to give Kate a pass to see me. It was just a matter of being persistent, but she finally got a pass. Then one of the nurses made arrangements to have only nurses who would be friendly to us come in to check on us. That was a huge help.*
>
> —CORY

5

What Will Raising Children Do to My Health?

While a lot has been written about a woman's health before and during pregnancy, it's almost impossible to find information about what happens to a woman's physical and mental health as she raises her children. After a woman has a baby, the mother's state of health, which was of central concern to friends, family, and her doctor for at least nine months, becomes almost invisible. Everyone around her tends to focus on the health and well-being of the baby instead.

Only recently, after a number of high-profile cases of mothers killing their children, have the media and more health professionals focused on a woman's mental health after pregnancy. But there is more to a mom's mental and physical health than postpartum depression and the healing of episiotomies. Many women experience an immense opening of their hearts to great possibilities and discover their own strength, tenacity, and ability to learn. They also face major physical changes and adjustments, especially in the early years.

Should I Breastfeed?

As exhilarating as having a new baby in the house can be, the early years of childrearing can also be traumatic to a woman's body. First she faces, if she chooses, the challenge of breastfeeding. She also faces the challenge of sifting through heaps of terribly inconsistent advice, usually delivered with passion and conviction from any number of sources.

The pediatrician was really pushing the breast milk thing. The baby nurse we hired made me feel terrible about the milk not coming in. The baby was crying. I should've just shut down that show, but I felt such pediatric pressure—the nurse, everybody said, "You gotta keep trying." In retrospect, I should've stopped, but I didn't know better. Everyone was mad at me when I added formula, but my baby was getting fed, and she felt better. It was four weeks of sheer hell.

—RAYNA

I had a very difficult time breastfeeding. It was just something I was single-minded about, and I was devastated at the thought that I would not be able to breastfeed. A lot of people were saying, "Give him a bottle, you're not a failure," but I was not going to do that. I found a lactation consultant and spent four weeks getting it going. Thinking back on it, I was really committed.

—MAGGIE

Once I threw all the rules out the window, nursed on demand, brought the baby into bed, held him when he wanted, it all became easier and more satisfying. Breastfeeding was good for me, good for him, and a lot less expensive than formula.

—DELORES

In spite of the saying "Breastfeeding is best feeding," it's only best feeding when it's mutually satisfying for mother and baby. Women who struggle with breastfeeding should feel comfortable converting to a bottle if they need to do so.

Will I Get Enough Sleep?

There is hardly a mother alive who won't testify to the lack of sleep she survived in the early years of her children's lives. College students and workers who pull double shifts can appreciate what a night without sleep does to motor skills, focus, and memory. Now multiply that times thirty, or ninety, for the first months of a newborn's life.

There is the occasional newborn who sleeps through the night almost immediately, but these babies are not the majority. Parents of newborns usually endure sleepless nights and days spent in a fog. They often try to function in what was their normal routine before the baby arrived, believing that they should be able to handle it. But sleep deprivation can have the same dangerous effects as being intoxicated. It can impair your concentration and the motor skills you need to drive a car, operate heavy machinery, or use sharp implements. Sleep deprivation in many people also shortens their fuse, leading to flashes of frustration and anger as well as bouts of depression.

I was so exhausted for so long that I felt totally defeated. I cut back my hours and closed a business after my second child.

—JOAN

I remember thinking that my baby would never get to be old enough for me to take him to the doctor for a checkup and see what I was doing wrong. I was tired all the time, up all night, depressed.

—ROXANNE

I let my body adapt during pregnancy. Getting up in the middle
of the night to pee isn't profoundly different than getting up in
the middle of the night to change a diaper or nurse a baby.
                                                          —SHANNON

Eventually, most healthy babies do sleep through the night, allowing the adults to return to a reasonable work schedule and daily routine.

My husband usually goes to work around 4:00 P.M. and is
home around midnight. He wakes up around 6:00 A.M., so we
have the morning together. When he goes back to work, we
won't have much time together, but he has Sundays and Mon-
days off, so we'll try to make Sundays just for us. We haven't
tried it yet, but we're going to try to have a date night, even if
we just go for a bike ride for a couple of hours.
                                                          —MELISSA

Parents can be enormously resourceful in avoiding sleep deprivation. The key is to make sure that both parents aren't awake in the middle of the night, so that one still has the energy for the daytime routine. Some couples put a bed in the baby's room, others assign the feedings in a way that gives each parent a period of uninterrupted sleep, and still others call in family members to help with the night shift.

Will I Be Able to Handle the Stress?

It's no surprise that women with children under age five suffer from a disproportionate rate of mental health problems. Yet it is often these women, working under the pressure of being a perfect mom, who struggle most to show the world they can handle it and so go untreated. Their partners are usually struggling with a new balance as well, so they may not notice the degree to which Mom is stressed and suffering. This stress can lead to depression, anxiety, domestic violence, child abuse, and more. In the most extreme cases, doctors and loved ones who fail to recognize or treat these symptoms of stress may end up witnessing a mother's demise or the demise of her children.

But most of us are not extreme cases. Stress comes in all degrees, from all directions, and in all forms. Some of it can be attributed to the sudden jolt you may feel in your daily routine, the introduction of a baby's crying into your household, the new disarray of your living space, or the steady stream of well-wishers who come through your door. Some women handle it by leaning heavily on the support their partners can provide, and some by calling on others to help. And there are always the old standbys for fighting stress: sleep and exercise.

I do make a concerted effort to get my daughter to bed by eight. I try to go to bed by 10:00 P.M., so there's a couple of hours there I can have to myself. When work is really busy, it gets bad because I have to spend those hours doing paperwork. I do sometimes have baby-sitters. Financially it's hard, and I have my parents who will take her for a night. My mother was trying to come on most Mondays, even though I didn't work, and she'd come for five hours so I could go to the gym or run errands, and that's really nice.

—SARA

It is totally amazing and you won't regret it, but you need help; a good support system is vital.

—HELEN

Can I Do All That Lifting?

While some women suffer back strain from pregnancy or musculoskeletal problems from difficult deliveries, an additional group of women suffer long-term back problems after the baby is born. First, their backs are often unprepared for the strain that the weight in their breasts from their milk coming in causes on their neck and upper back. At the same time, their back is taking on the new weight of carrying the newborn.

As the baby grows, your lower back begins to take the brunt of the abuse, as you try to maneuver the diaper bag and the infant, bending over into the backseat of the car to reach the car seat or folding the stroller and lifting it into the trunk with one hand while holding the baby in the other. Careful and proper lifting, along with stretching to relieve spasms, can help alleviate the pain.

> *I never knew such back pain! There were days I could only take little baby steps, I had to crawl to the bathroom, and I couldn't imagine picking up my daughter. I kept wishing she'd learn how to walk sooner! That was a tough time, and I've only had sporadic trouble since then.*
>
> —DARLENE

Can Motherhood Be Good for My Mental Health?

In these early years, moms—and dads as well—find themselves enjoying a new perspective on the world. You have made the transition to a developmental stage that takes you beyond caring for your own needs to caring for someone else's. You must now anticipate the needs of someone who cannot articulate them. Sometimes, as your children grow older, you take on a new appreciation for the role model you are becoming, and you pay extra attention to your language and actions.

Some parents are absolutely euphoric about this new role. They can be heard in conversation or read on E-mail message boards, elated with their baby's latest accomplishment and thrilled with their ability to have an impact on such a tiny being. It can be quite a rush, and it's very much a part of the attraction to motherhood for many women.

> *I think I feel really needed and loved. I have grown up a lot in the last ten years and have a completely different outlook on life, one that is much healthier and much more fulfilling.*
>
> —CARLA

> *I am a much nicer, kinder person now. I feel fulfilled as a parent when I see my son laugh, learn a new skill, or pass a milestone.*
>
> —TINA

What if I Have a Child with Disabilities?

Another surprise prospective parents may have to face is the chance that their child will be born with or will develop disabilities. For instance, the older you are, the higher the chances that your child will suffer chromosomal defects. The same goes in families with known risks for genetic defects.

Moms, who often assume the heaviest responsibilities of caring for their disabled child, need to make time for themselves and take good care of their own health. Stress, sleep deprivation, and backaches are some of the common motherhood health issues that can be magnified for a mother of a child with disabilities. You would have to learn to allow your partner to take over duties, trust family members to cover for an afternoon, or bring in professional respite care.

> She became sick at two months old. It turned out to be a rare bone disease, osteopetrosis. Both my mom and stepmom, dad and stepdad, and sister have all been there. I pray a lot. I talk to friends, family, boyfriend, and let my frustrations out. A home health care nurse does respite for me, takes her every Tuesday night and sometimes overnight. Teachers come into the home regularly (in addition to school). The music therapist, doctors, and other families at the hospital—we've always been there for one another.
>
> —JAIMI

Parents of children with disabilities find themselves juggling the full-time job of dealing with doctors, public and private agencies, school districts, and their personal finances in addition to the rest of their daily routine. How will you feel if confronted by this news? Do you have the strength, confidence, and desire to address the needs your child will have? How will you feel if your health or genetic makeup is the cause of your child's disabilities?

> *Despite the feeling of failure or guilt I have for bringing life into the world that had so many challenges to face, I think going through all the experiences with both children has strengthened me.*
>
> —MARGARET

> *I work with children with disabilities, and at the time I got pregnant at forty-two, I was working in a neonatal intensive care unit, exposed to babies with problems. I felt anxious about it. But the main thing at my age was the risk for chromosomal abnormalities. I told very few people until I had my amniocentesis. I think I would have terminated the pregnancy if I thought there was a problem. Sometimes you just don't know, but I was very anxious.*
>
> —ALICE

6

What Does Having Children Do to a Relationship?

Romantic relationships are built on many interpersonal interactions, and almost every relationship, at one level or another, employs the art of negotiation. Two people attracted to one another may negotiate anything from where they should meet for a date to whether to spend the night together. But the decision about whether or not to bring a baby into the relationship can be the most challenging negotiations a couple ever navigates.

And the negotiations don't end with settling the question of whether or not to have children, to adopt, to get an abortion, or to pursue fertility treatments. In fact, they only begin. Every step of the way, the couple will need to reassess their approach to the child. It could start in pregnancy with who will become the primary caretaker, then move to what is the best method of discipline, religious training, world outlook, and eventually whether Junior is ready to have the car keys. This kind of discussion can strengthen a relationship in ways you never could have anticipated, or it can introduce tensions that you never expected would surface.

How Do We Talk About Kids?

In all negotiations, it is important to state your needs clearly, listen well, be prepared for changes in initial positions, and agree on the resolution. Couples who can approach each set of negotiations as a team effort, with the same goals in mind, can become very successful partners in love, in life, and in parenthood (if they so decide).

Women choose different times to raise the issue of children with their love interest. Usually, it comes up during the dating phase, but amazingly, sometimes it doesn't surface until much later.

> He always joked around that I'd change my mind and want kids, but he never pushed for it or expressed an interest in it. I had to have a hysterectomy, and he left six months later. He now has two children. I wish he'd been clearer about that from the start.
>
> —JO

As women who want children get older, they often bring the issue up very early in a dating relationship. They see no point wasting time with someone who doesn't want the same thing they do.

> The minute I met Gary, I was on him to have a baby. I met him when I was thirty-four. I had already selected the best in vitro guys here as my normal gynecologists, because I knew I was getting up there. I was plannin' ahead, baby!
>
> —LENA

Younger women we talked to had often put off the conversation. They either relied on certain assumptions (never a safe bet) or were afraid to introduce the subject.

> *Before we got married, we didn't discuss it. I had to bang him*
> *on the head about it. If we're going to do this, we have to do it*
> *now. I knew this would be right for him. I knew it was just*
> *anxiety, that this would change his life and he'd be thrilled.*
> *And once he said OK, he was great. He was thrilled that I was*
> *pregnant. He was on board. If he had said no, I would have*
> *dealt with it somehow. That's how I am.*
>
> —MARGI

Women are socialized to please others. If you can put aside what other people want and make this decision based on your own needs and desires, you will more likely be laying a much stronger foundation for your relationship. Sharing a life with the one you love is a series of compromises that may mean delaying your goals for a while in order to support your partner's goals. But on the issue of motherhood, compromise can be dangerous. Having children is an all-consuming, all-or-nothing proposition that can destroy a marriage if not taken seriously.

> *He told me he wanted to have a couple of kids, and I would've*
> *been fine without them, but he wanted them, so I did it for*
> *him. I was depressed for a long time. I got pregnant with my*
> *third that I didn't want in any way, shape, or form. Then my*
> *oldest got diabetes. I hadn't really wanted the second one*
> *either. We lived in a trailer. Everything we had was crap. The*
> *last thing I needed was another baby.*
>
> —CATHY

> *We don't have that same kind of shared time we had exclu-*
> *sively before Tracy, but there's a common understanding that*
> *this was part of the deal.*
>
> —REBECCA

Will We Be Able to Hear Each Other?

Listening to your partner is just as important as stating what you need. That skill requires time, experience, and conscious development. It is more than just hearing what a person is saying; it's understanding what your partner means and, many times, noticing what your partner is *not* saying. It's watching what your partner does with the information you give.

> *When the subject of kids came up, he would never be real clear about whether he wanted them or not. He'd just say, "Wait and see." He didn't seem to enjoy being around kids much. He never talked about his childhood. After a few years of trying to talk to him about it, I realized that even if he was never going to come out and say it, he really didn't want any children.*
>
> —NINA

Good negotiators know how to listen well, which often means asking follow-up questions or repeating what the other person has just stated to fully understand what he or she is trying to say. Couples can avoid many a misunderstanding by developing this skill. At first it can seem very contrived, but like learning to drive a stick shift; after a while, you don't even notice you're doing it, but the ride gets much smoother.

What if We Change Our Minds?

Career path and progress, social life, a particular romantic relationship, aging, the death of a parent—and for some adopted children, the discovery of their birth parents—are just some of the life-altering events that can change your perspective on having children.

> *We're usually fine about not having kids, but my husband lost his dad last year, and he gets sad when he thinks of the son he doesn't have.*
>
> —ALEX

Then there is the situation where one person in the couple is ready to commit to the relationship, but not (yet) to having children.

> *I always made it known I wanted to have at least two children. He has a child from a previous relationship and wasn't quite so sure that was something he needed to experience again. Even though we were disagreeing, I had a sense he'd be more open to that once he was done with school and had a steady job. Slowly he's come around now. I wasn't open to pursuing the relationship if he wasn't willing to talk about it more. If he became dead set against it, I'd have to leave.*
>
> —SALLY

Sometimes there is no single event that causes the change of mind. Most long-term relationships have been established on a particular set of expectations. If only one of you experiences a change of mind, the relationship will have to adjust. For example, if you come to realize that one wants children and the other doesn't, discussing it or working with a counselor will be helpful. Many times the common ground that you find on so many other levels is also the common ground you will come to share regarding children.

> *He really wanted children, and I think this whole infertility thing has been a real disappointment to him. But every once in a while, he'll turn to me and say, "I'm glad we don't have children." The stressful part was that section when we were trying to get pregnant, not that section after when we decided to create a life without children. That was when we could let go.*
>
> —JACOLE

> *During that time, our lives kept going on. We have good lives and good friends, and over a couple of months, I just started thinking how great my life was and how I liked my life and how much things would change with a baby. Did I really want my life to change that much when I was already really happy? . . . We'd given things so much thought, we'd forgotten the reason why we were doing it. We'd thought about all the hows and how-tos and forgotten about the purpose.*
>
> —TERRI

What if We Can't Agree About Kids?

If you find yourselves on opposite sides of negotiations most of the time and for long periods of time, facing an opponent who doesn't respect or listen to your opinion or simply cannot agree with you, then you need to reconsider the relationship.

> *He was much older than I was. He kept saying that he knew I'd want children someday, and I kept telling him I had never, ever had the desire to bear children. It was like he couldn't believe it, or he didn't hear me. I offered to call off the wedding, but he said we couldn't; the invitations had already been sent. As stupid as that sounds now, I let it be the excuse that kept us going forward, probably doomed from the start.*
>
> —JONI

> *He didn't want to have children, so I was afraid my pregnancy would alienate him (which it eventually did). We discussed abortion, but he was adamantly opposed to it. I also thought starting out our marriage by aborting a pregnancy we created would be a bad start, although I'd had an abortion a few years earlier. No amount of discussion brought us to mutual agreement or compromise. He finally just gave in to me.*
>
> —SARA-JANE

The discussion about children, just like having children, can bring out many differences between a couple, sometimes including some disturbing dynamics in how you relate to one another. This is a good time to listen to your gut, set aside the convenience of that particular relationship or the amount of time and energy you've expended on it, and think seriously about whether or not to take it indefinitely into the future. Carefully assess the kind of commitment you're making to each other. If the question of children is up in the air, it might be best for you to hold off making a lifelong commitment until you see if one or the other changes positions.

What if We Can't Get Pregnant?

Couples' hopes and aspirations face devastation when they begin to suspect that pregnancy won't be as easy as they'd always assumed it would be. Tensions begin to escalate, and you may begin to feel desperate with the rigors of timing intercourse. Your partner may begin to feel impotent, both figuratively and literally. Both of you begin to suffer declining self-esteem, which can escalate the cycle of desperation.

Amazingly, still today, the medical profession and others often assume that infertility is caused by some problem with the woman when, in fact, in 40 percent of couples, it's the man. Although it's less common these days, women occasionally have extensive fertility workups, including laparoscopy, while their male partners never even submit a sperm count. You should always request your doctor do a sperm count before moving on to more invasive diagnostic procedures on you.

Infertility brings a flood of emotional issues that couples are often ill-equipped to handle. Here are some ways a couple can cope with this often lengthy, expensive, and traumatic life event:

- Reaffirm your love, sexuality, and attraction to each other often.
- Be involved in the infertility treatments as a team, so that one does not drift away from the other or make it into "her" project.
- Continue to reassess your goals in life. Sometimes that which we can't have is what we want the most. Is it possible that knowing you can't have a baby, easily at least, is making you more driven to get one than you otherwise would be?

- Watch out for the drugs. Some fertility drugs have side effects on a woman's mood. Women with mood disorders should be particularly careful to have their fertility doctor consult with their psychiatrist.
- Be ready for heartbreak. After investing $10,000 or more on one effort at in vitro fertilization, a woman can be devastated at seeing her period begin. Couples need to support each other more than ever during such difficult times.
- Be prepared for the loss of intimacy that comes with escalating fertility interventions. Science objectifies what many believe is a sacred act —creating life. Couples who decide that high-tech is worth it because they want a baby that badly should be prepared for the scientific necessity of medical staff's poking and prodding. Many women report feeling humiliated by the process and suffer a sense of loss of control over their bodies.
- Decide whether this will be a private or public struggle. Couples who decide to share their troubles with their inner circle of friends should be prepared for those friends becoming intimately aware of the woman's cycles and calling monthly to see if she started her period.

It's destructive to some marriages, but it strengthened ours. It probably had a negative sexual effect. "Have sex at this time, have sex in this position" takes all the spontaneity and fun out of it. We never fully recovered from that, but I don't know if that's the way it is in normal life when you have a baby, go back to work, get fat and middle-aged and ugly.

—NIKKI

I had to be very open about the in vitro process. My team at that point was very tight, and we were having a lot of trials, so I had to be completely open about it, or they would have thought I had cancer with all the visits to the doctor. So I had seven people by the door every time, asking, "How many eggs? When's the transfer?" If we hadn't hit a home run, there would have been seven people who aren't close friends that I would've had to share that with.

—TERESA

We considered in vitro, and I got as far as making an appointment. They sent me this twenty-page questionnaire to fill out before the appointment. I sat down to fill it out, all excited, but by the time I got to the end of it, I decided I wasn't going to do it. I was in tears and totally devastated. There were so many questions in there that seemed picky and irrelevant. If this is what they need to know to find out whether or not I can have children, there is something wrong with the universe.

—DEBBIE

This is a complex problem. If you find yourself struggling with infertility, we encourage you to confer with experts. A good place to start is with the national infertility group RESOLVE: The National Infertility Association (resolve.com). Another website that will refer you to other organizations is Internet Health Resources, at ihr.com/infertility/organize.html.

How Would We Divide the Parenting?

Negotiations between two adults continue as prospective parents begin to imagine life with a baby. A good exercise, not to mention a way of understanding more about your partner, is to have each of you take a separate piece of paper and write down who you think will perform each baby-related task. Here are some you can start with or discuss:

- Who will stay home with the baby, and for how long?
- Whose career will wait or end, or just proceed at a slower pace?
- Who will take the baby to the doctor?
- Who will drop off and pick up the child from day care?
- Who will stay home when child care falls through or the child is sick?
- Who will get up in the middle of the night when the baby cries?
- Who will change the diapers?
- Who will make sure that baby supplies, such as diapers or formula, are fully stocked?
- Who will arrange play dates with other kids?
- Who will research preschools, day-care centers, or summer camps when needed?
- Who will be responsible for keeping house?
- Who will prepare food for the baby?
- Who will cook our meals?
- Who will do the baby's laundry and be sure she always has clean clothes available?
- Who will speak to the grandparents when there's an issue with them?

I can't say that I enjoyed the very young children at all. My husband was really great about helping with them then. He loved those years and enjoyed the children more when they were babies than I did. I felt consumed by the children. Then in the later years, I enjoyed the children more. My husband and I changed roles.

—ANNIE

I began to feel unfairly burdened. I always got up in the night because he had to get up early to go to work. I did all the dirty work. I became lonely for adult company because when he came home from work, he was tired and wanted to retreat into his study to unwind alone. I felt like a single parent much of the time.

—KATRINA

Same-sex couples must tackle additional role issues related to your alternative lifestyle. For instance, gay men must face the struggle of their limited access to adoption services and the likelihood that they will adopt a child with special needs. Lesbians using donor insemination may face fluctuating roles as one or both decide they would like to have the pregnancy and birth experience, and the negotiations continue as they decide who will be primary caretaker and for how long.

I always wanted kids, but Sandi had never thought much about it. We had no idea what she would do, if she wanted to make that sacrifice. The first year, it was up in the air. The question was whether or not she would stay in the relationship, not whether or not we'd be equal partners. Now we divide roles by competence and preference. We both work outside the home, but I enjoy a lot of traditional homemaking chores, so she takes on jobs she doesn't necessarily like doing—to keep it equal.

—MOLLY

Could We Survive Baby Boot Camp?

Most couples anticipating raising children can hardly make it past the pristine images of happy moms pushing strollers full of content babies, proud parents passing off the quiet newborn to even prouder grandparents, and the joyful looks of parents at the coffee shop as their little one practices her first steps.

Life with a new baby is full of joyous, unforgettable moments. Still, there is something about the power a newborn has over its parents that is transfixing and exhausting at the same time. Life with newborns is very much like "baby boot camp"—you're in it because you love it, but it's going to challenge you at every turn.

When you bring a newborn baby into your home, you are signing up for a routine in which someone less competent than you is in charge. That person orders you around with complete disregard for your needs, such as sleep or nutrition, and that person never ever lets up, ever. Boot camp is intended to mold the recruit into somebody who can function automatically, without thinking, and that's exactly what your baby will do—to you!

> *I had all these notions—I would do photo albums, some career work while I was off on maternity leave. It took me forever just to send out thank-you notes, and that bothered me. I try to be good about that stuff.*
>
> —MARIA

The primary caretaker suffers the brunt of boot camp, while the working parent gets out on furlough to go to work. The good news is that during most baby boot camps, couples don't usually break down at the same time. The other good news is that eventually your baby sleeps through the night, takes the breast or a bottle easily, and even sometimes takes scheduled naps. Until then, though, the primary caretaker is better off assuming that there is no predicting what the day will hold and letting this time be spent on resting and caring for the baby.

I have a totally modern, 50 percent husband, but somehow early on, we established that I was the night person, even after we switched to bottles. He's a much heavier sleeper. To this day I haven't slept through her crying through the monitor. I wake up immediately. He's the one still getting up to go to the office, so I should be the night person, but then in the day, I found it impossible to nap because it felt like I had a million things to do.

—PAM

How Will We Handle "Honey, I'm Home"?

In the first few months of parenthood, designated breadwinners often come home feeling guilty and anxious about their partner and their baby. As they walk in and perhaps see the exhausted, irritable, frustrated partner they love but hardly recognize, they'll feel clueless about how to make it better. (If new parents aren't careful, that guilt can sometimes translate into letting the baby's routine slide—keeping him up late to play, for instance—that can lead to later problems with the baby's behavior.)

When your baby is first born, the two of you will be joined together in a common cause. You'll both be learning new skills like holding, bathing, and diapering the baby. You'll probably both get excited by the subtle changes and sudden growth in your baby. But if one of you goes off to work and one stays home, that cause won't be so common anymore. After about five to six weeks, most couples experience this strange feeling of jealousy creeping in. It's a common and yet most unexpected feeling. Your baby (who will just be starting to respond to the world) and the stay-at-home parent are sharing experiences that the working parent misses.

If you're the one who goes back to work and leaves your partner home with the baby, this feeling can be even more acutely painful. You're still carrying with you all those societal expectations of motherhood. That long-running dialogue is still going in your mind: "How can I call myself a good mother if I'm not home for my baby?" Meanwhile, the stay-at-home parent is thinking, "Hey, you get to leave and get a break from this." The jealousy tends to run both ways. If you deal with it up front and quickly, it can strengthen your relationship and improve the way you both are coping with your new situation. Left untended, it can cause resentment and possibly harm the relationship.

> *We don't know any other families where the female is the working person and the father is giving child care, so I think in our house it's much different. We're kind of creating our own destiny. Before she was born, I cooked, cleaned, did laundry, cleaned up cat puke. This arrangement gave me new perspective on him because he devoted himself to her. They're best buddies. At one point she didn't want to have anything to do with me, and that felt horrible. So now as a couple, we've decided to have her spend more time with me, and that's helped.*
>
> —ANDY

> *Though my spouse claimed to be committed to our relationship, his commitment and love for me faded quickly after our child was born. He was jealous of the baby, did not find me sexually attractive anymore, and in general, acted like a baby himself. He verbally and emotionally abused me and refused to go to counseling.*
>
> —SONDRA

Will There Be Time for a Reality Check?

Not long after the baby comes, you'll see whether you both accurately predicted your roles and routines. Maybe you thought Dad would be the one to wake up for the baby at night, but you discover Dad has become a heavy sleeper, so now Mom gets up. Maybe the working parent thought the one at home would be the one keeping the house clean, but getting home from work has turned into a journey through an obstacle course of baby toys, unmade beds, scattered shoes, half-used diaper rags, and dirty dishes.

As soon as the baby is sleeping through the night, you both can sit down and look over your old lists of expectations:

- How are you feeling?
- Is it working out the way you'd planned?
- Are both of you satisfied with the daily routine and duties you're performing?
- Do you need to do some sorting and shifting to ease the stress for either of you?

This is your turn at a reality check. If you take the time to have this conversation and make the necessary adjustments, you increase the chances that you will both be able to focus more happily on your child and each other. Your childrearing once again becomes an ever-evolving project for both of you, a continuing manifestation of your love.

*I think there were a lot of scared feelings. Can I do this? How
will we work together? Will the workload be shared? We share
work pretty well, but at home we're fairly traditional. How
much is he going to help with this process? How am I going to
do this? Am I going to get enough help from him in doing this?
It is an ongoing struggle. I don't think there's a lot of conflict,
but there is tension around who's going to do what. Who's
going to take the kids to school today?*

—SARAH

*It was 1988 to '89, and there was no negotiating. I did it. I
would take care of the kids, and I would go to work. I had to
take them to the sitter every day; my husband did nothing.
Even though he's the one that wanted them. I just bit my
tongue. I didn't want to be alone. All my life I wanted to be
married; that meant you were a good person or something.*

—EILEEN

*David is on leave and is doing most of the domestic chores
right now. I do clean and tidy, but he washes floors, cooks.
When he goes back to work, we probably won't eat as well and
will probably rely on the deli. We're OK with that for now. I can
see when the second baby comes me taking more time off than
I did this time, for sure.*

—JASMINE

Will We Still Want to Make Love?

Postpartum is often a difficult time for romance. In addition to the physical changes we discussed earlier, the woman is experiencing a dramatic role change from lover to mother.

> *My relationship changed much more than I thought it would. I went from feeling like a lover to feeling like a mother, and nothing else was as important as my daughter.*
>
> —JEANETTE

> *It's hard not to get bored when you know you have to wait until the child goes to sleep and then sex is next. I sometimes feel like my passion is on hold until 8:00 P.M. We can't just make love when the moment hits anymore, and sometimes after a long day and after dealing with your child, all you want to do is just relax and focus on yourself.*
>
> —MAUREEN

Energy also is always a factor. After surviving a day of baby boot camp, sex becomes just another form of exercise, and Mom usually doesn't have the energy. As far as she's concerned, those highly valued moments when baby isn't crying are best spent sleeping!

Men face a different challenge. The new dad has just seen (or imagined, if he wasn't in the room) six to eight pounds of baby passing through the place where he has experienced, until now, only carnal pleasure. At night, as he's trying to woo you, you're suddenly distracted by a sound coming from the baby. Your partner may feel rejected because of your exhaustion, and he may feel impatient because of the time it takes for you to heal from childbirth. His opportunity to feel rejected increases as you devote all of your time and energy to the baby. It's a new perspective, sometimes one that can squash libido like a bug or make that bug crawl elsewhere.

> *Our romantic relationship did not change much for me, but it gave my husband more time to pursue his outside romantic interests. I was doing all the parenting; that kept me occupied.*
> —BONNIE

The patterns that parents establish during this first year will likely persist as the child or children grow older. If these patterns are harmful, they will continue to cause problems in the relationship. If they are healthy, they will enhance the adult relationship as well as the relationship between the parents and the children.

How Much Time Do We Need for the Two of Us?

Couples with children have less time with each other alone. And when they get that time alone, it can often feel more like an appointment, or at best a date, than like the lifetime they signed up for.

The adult relationship in a family needs extra special nurturing—the intentional night out, the planned dinner date, or the early alarm clock ring for cuddling time. Women can be very quick to sense when their partner is drifting away into other interests or more deeply into work and career. And sometimes it's the stay-at-home-mom, with her new full-time career as mother and newly found expertise with the baby, who fades away from the mutual interests of the couple. If you decide to have children, you'll need time to regularly renew your own relationship, touch base with each other on adult matters, and remember who you were before you were parents. That often means limiting dinner conversation to a quick update on what the baby did today, then finding out what happened at work for your partner. This is not to imply a 1950s-style notion about what topics of conversation are more interesting than others. It is, instead, an important exercise in taking time to have an adult relationship by balancing the conversation between baby news and other interests.

As your infant grows older, you may decide to take vacations without the baby. You won't ruin your kid if you do it, but you could ruin yourselves if you don't.

When the youngest entered full-day school, we tried to begin to connect again, but it was extremely difficult.

—KENDRA

The kids are like the whole relationship. They have a huge effect. When we talk, it's about the kids or what we need to do for the kids or where we'll run the kids. Our lives are revolving around our children. He has a lot more freedom, but he's always home at six when I get home, so we can deal with the kids together. He hates being alone to deal with them, but so do I.

—CARLYLE

Couples deciding whether or not to have children should consider whether you are willing to give up that exclusive claim you have on each other, that intimate and expansive amount of time you spend alone together after work or on weekends, the flexibility you have for scheduling vacations, and the other stolen moments you now enjoy.

My husband said he had not really thought about it, but once we had talked, he realized he had never thought seriously about having children of his own. He's very content being childless. He wanted to do other things with his life. We're in our forties, and we mountain bike. We couldn't do that with children.

—JOYCE

My time, devotion, and attention were redirected away from my partner and toward my son. But I also saw my partner in a new light—a caring father—being attentive to my son's needs. That made me love and respect my husband on a new, deeper level.

—DANA

Will the "Little" Things Get Too Big?

Bringing a child into the house is like raising a giant magnifying glass over the personalities of the two adults in the family and their relationship. Whatever used to annoy you about your partner will annoy you ten times more after the baby is born. It's not the baby's fault, and it's not even your partner's fault; it's what sleep deprivation and all of these other stresses naturally do to a relationship.

On the positive side, the experience can reveal strengths and qualities in your partner you never knew about, and your partner may gain a profound respect for you in your new role. On the negative side, most couples have no way of predicting which of their magnified idiosyncrasies will turn into insurmountable obstacles.

> *I wasn't prepared for how much my [ex-]husband was going to become like his father, how little he was going to help, how we would not have the same needs. We dealt with it by screaming and by deciding I was the problem and by not sleeping. We finally dealt with it by separating.*
>
> —MARIA

The latest divorce rates among couples with children testify to the fact that having children certainly does not keep couples together. Women who have divorced have firm advice for women considering motherhood.

Talk, talk, talk to your partner. Make sure your ideas about religion, work, money, chores are similar. If they truly don't want to be a parent, having a child with them will probably not change their mind. Make sure, if you go that route, you're prepared to be a single mom raising a child alone.

—LANETT

As you contemplate motherhood, you may want to consider your ability and your partner's ability to let go of things that aggravate you, because as fun as children are, aggravation will definitely become part of the mix.

I would count the minutes before he'd get home for supper. He'd always been a little late for things, but every night now, I'd watch the clock, and my heart would sink. The baby would be fussing. I'd think, "There's no way I'm going to make it through another meal with this boy alone." Then he'd call. Work was running late. Someone walked in, and he had to deal with it. I just wanted to scream. Sometimes I did. Why couldn't he just get home on time for once?

—KATHLEEN

Talking to each other, finding the comedy in the situation, and having a few laughs help couples survive. At more serious times, you can remind each other of the love you feel, why you came together, and the pleasurable traits you admire in each other.

Every time his parents came to visit, his mom would truck in loads of food, and his dad would get to work fixing something in the house. At first I thought it was this huge insult to my cooking and our house maintenance abilities. I was really hurt. But after the first few times, when he saw that look coming over my face, my husband would just take my hand and walk me out the door. We'd go have a date—to a movie, a walk in the park, a cup of coffee. It was wonderful.

—HETTI

Will It Get Any Easier on Us?

The newborn period is probably the toughest time on couples, but as your children get older, they provide new challenges for the two of you. Here are some highlights:

INFANTS

As we've discussed, during your child's infancy, you are both adapting to the fact that someone in your household requires full-time care. It isn't easy, and it doesn't end in the first few months.

> *I was surprised how much energy it takes to be with a baby twenty-four hours a day, seven days a week.*
>
> —ANNE

TODDLERS

The toddler stage is one of the most amazing, as your baby begins to look and act like "a real person." Your baby's personality starts to shine in a way that can make you stare in amazement and pride, but also in ways that can try your patience to no end. Toddlers are learning to assert themselves, and the adults have to be consistent in their responses. Again, you may have to negotiate issues of discipline, bedtime, and other challenges. Kids seem to be born with the ability to play the "permissive" one against the "disciplinarian" and vice versa. And just keeping up with your newly self-propelled toddler can wear you to a frazzle.

*The most gratifying is all the things they learn. You're just
filling their brains with all kinds of stuff. It's just amazing how
they soak it up. They look at you and say, "What's next?" They
do soak it up, even if it's swear words, and they're ready to go.*

—PATTY

*Run, run, run after them. I hated changing diapers. I hated
dragging a kid with me everywhere I went. So I just stayed
home. I didn't want to go out to eat because he'd cause a scene
and I'd have to leave anyway. I hated bothering other people
with my kid in public, so I just didn't go anywhere after a
while.*

—JANIE

*Oh, I thought I had all the patience in the world. Wrong! He's a
terror in disguise. Try doing your makeup and watching him.
Oops! He got your lipstick and has ruined your comforter!
Damn! Running late! Now where are the keys? I used to hang
them up . . . oh, yeah, I let him chew on them since he's
teething and cranky!*

—VEDA

SCHOOL-AGE CHILDREN

When children reach age five or so, they are rapidly learning responsibility, and you get a break as the kids go off to school. At the same time,
parents must agree on discipline, religion, interpretations of human
behavior, manners, encouraging a child's talents, communicating with
the school, finding experts to help challenged children, and more.

*This age is a beautiful time. They are cooperative, loving and
think you walk on water.*

—KERRI

*As they get older, they need me more for activities than they
did when they were younger. That's been a surprise. I thought
when they were older, they'd be on their own; they can dress*

themselves. But they really need me a lot. I help with their Girl Scouts, I'm on the advisory board with their school, and they really like that and want my involvement. They need me more, and they're old enough to verbalize.

—MANDY

ADOLESCENCE

Teens require more supervision than younger children, which often surprises parents. At the same time, that supervision requires much more finesse. Just as with full-grown adults, encouragement, respect, and good communication can make living with a teen a positive experience and strengthen your relationship with your child. Humiliating, embarrassing, or getting into power struggles with teens can harm your relationship and shut them off from you.

Teens are even better than younger children at playing parents against one another, so parents need to communicate with each other more than ever. You will each probably "let go" at different rates; one will permit a longer curfew than another, for instance. One or both of you may be confronted by choices you made at that age and later regretted. Presenting a united front is more important now than ever because the potential for damage is much greater. Your ability to work well together to solve problems will become apparent as your teen tries to test every limit.

As my oldest son got older, they locked horns a lot. My husband was from another era and expected a certain level of obeying and structure that felt very strange and unnatural to me. He'd lay down certain laws and disappear, and I'd be working (at home) but wasn't supposed to let them watch TV. I didn't know what to do.

—CINDY

I swear the aliens take your child away during this time. You wake up and wonder, "Who are these people?" All I could do was brace myself, read my Bible, pray, and try not to kill them!

—LYNN

You will very likely be in for some serious surprises—both wonderful and incredibly difficult.

—JACKIE

I watched them come into adolescence and turn into something nasty and rude. My philosophy is freeze 'em at twelve, thaw them out at twenty-five so you don't have to go through all that stuff with them. They have to do it in a frozen state.

—NATALIE

What if the Marriage Breaks Up?

No woman reading this book expects to get divorced, but we must be honest about the statistics. While no one goes into marriage planning to end it, about one in two couples divorce.

But we plan our lives as if this could never happen to us, which is not all bad, unless it happens. Most couples don't negotiate prenuptial agreements, against the advice of every major money adviser in the country, and women with children risk ending up with less income than when they were married.

Women on the other side of the divorce experience are consistent in their advice: "Go into having children expecting you might have to raise them alone."

> I didn't have the maturity to look at the overall picture. "What if this happens or that happens?" It wasn't well thought out; it was just the thing to do, the escape. I never thought, "Could I take care of this child on my own?" I would have waited until I had better skills and better financial means to support them on my own.
>
> —BRENDA

It's unromantic and cynical, but it does no harm to consider the possibility. Spend just a few moments in the position of a woman going through a divorce, and see the difference between a woman with children and a woman without:

A woman without children will have to divide her belongings with her partner. You will have to find a lawyer to process the divorce. You will have to find a new place to live, unless your partner moves out, and it will likely be smaller and less expensive, since you are no longer sharing income. You can move anywhere in the country to find a job if you need to. And when the divorce is final, you will never have to see your partner again.

A woman with children will also have to divide her belongings with her partner, but if the partner wants to stay actively involved in the children's lives, some belongings will stay in both households. The majority of women divorced today have primary custody of the children, but they have less income. Your partner may or may not pay child support, so when you hire a lawyer, it will be not only for the divorce but the child custody negotiations and possibly child support enforcement. Your children will be in both lives, so you will be forever connected to your partner and to the way that partner organizes his life. That may mean trusting your children to a stepmom you may not think is trustworthy or dealing with long-distance relationships between the children and your ex. Your relationship may remain amicable, which is the best scenario, or you may develop an angry or hate-filled relationship that is difficult for all parties. If you leave a relationship thinking you never want to see him again, that won't be possible until your children are grown.

> *Someone once said that the purpose of joint custody is so that once a week you remember why you left. That saying hasn't failed me yet!*
>
> —DARLA

> *All three were with me the first six months, living in poverty. I had no skills, no job. His lawyer had instructed him not to give me a dime. It took forever for the first checks to arrive, and I was no budgeter. I was scared to death. If the kids went to live with their dad, I'd have no worries, they'd be well provided for. I didn't think about their emotional health. At different times, their stepmother would get out of control with one child or another. That was a problem.*
>
> —BRANDI

Are Stepmothers Moms, Too?

Women who decide to marry partners who have children from a previous relationship are also making the decision to become mothers. While it is likely the children will stay with their biological mother most of the time, many fathers are actively involved in the lives of their children after divorce. That may mean one-week-on, one-week-off custody, phone calls every night, weekends with the kids, and extra rooms in the house dedicated to the children's intermittent use. Stepparenting is rife with complications we cannot address here, but bookshelves and the Internet are chock full of advice and support.

Women who know that they can't have children but want them are often attracted to a man with children. You may be disappointed in the limited time you will spend with the children and the limited impact you'll have on them, especially if the biological mother has primary custody.

Some women who never wanted children downplay the fact that their new fellow comes as a package deal with his children. In this situation, you may feel like the time and energy he spends with his kids are an intrusion on your relationship. You might be surprised if the children treat you rudely, but most children secretly want their parents to get back together and consider stepmoms a major obstacle in their quest.

> My stepson is so out of control! They've had him to therapists and shrinks, on meds and not on meds. I set limits, but his father says I'm too harsh. He won't listen to the professionals, neither does the biological mom, and the kid runs wild. We can't get two minutes alone together when he's with us, and

I'm so tired afterwards that I'm not sure I want to see his father
much anyway.

—ARLENE

Finally, women who are stepping into the place of a mother who died have an enormous task ahead of them. A stepmother in this situation is trying to show the children that she is not trying to replace Mom. Since the widower usually has sole responsibility for the children, you at least get a better sense from the outset of the challenges you face. Women entering into such relationships have to recognize that children complicate relationships. They can enrich them beyond measure, or they can exacerbate problems between the adults that you never thought were significant.

At the beginning there were times I felt like I'd never be a real
part of the family. They have such rich memories of their mom,
and who am I to say anything? When they'd sit around and
talk about her, I would just keep quiet. Now I ask questions
about her, show interest, and that gets them talking more. It
seems to help.

—AMANDA

7

Will the Village Be There When I Need It?

The old African proverb "It takes an entire village to raise a child" was made famous in the United States when Senator Hillary Clinton, then First Lady, used it as a title for her book discussing the social responsibility we all have in raising the nation's children.

In a broad sense, we have always needed a village to raise our children. In the preindustrial United States, large farm families living near one another helped raise the children, who grew quickly into their responsibilities on the farm. This remained true even longer in southern states and among African-Americans, where much of that larger community remains or is reconstructed in larger cities today.

These days our "villages" take on many forms—as cities, suburbs, rural communities, and even phone-line or online communities. The members of the community you'll be joining if you have children represent a vast network on which to rely when you need assistance. If you decide not to have children, you will find a growing community of child-free singles and couples as well.

Will My Peers Be Able to Help?

Women preparing for childbirth often take classes offered by the local hospital or clinic. There they find other women waddling in the signature walk of pregnant women, wondering when this fascinating, frustrating, and fickle being will release itself from their bodies. They all are feeling the same fears, anxieties, joys, and anticipation. They look around the room at each other, feeling not so alone, hoping to make a few new friends.

Unfortunately, these women will soon have newborn infants, too, so they won't be able to come over and baby-sit. Even so, they are great to talk to on the phone and commiserate with, so you know you're not alone.

> *I barely knew Kristi, but we had exchanged phone numbers in childbirth class. I'm so glad we did. We would talk on the phone like old girlfriends about diapers, breastfeeding, sex— you name it!*
>
> —COLLEEN

This is not to say all women who have just given birth disappear. Mothers who don't work outside their home have more time and often reach out to other new moms in the neighborhood. For women in the workforce, many yoga centers have evening classes, and some new-mother groups may meet in the evenings as well.

On their own, new moms may have a hard time managing more than a nap and the dishes—but in urban and suburban areas, local hospitals, clinics, and religious and community centers often host new-mom support groups. The struggle can be just getting to them, but there you can find other women coping with the same feelings of inadequacy, lack of control, and sleep deprivation common among all new mothers.

If you can't get out but have Internet access, you can find support, guidance, and a place to voice your frustrations on various bulletin boards and in chat rooms. After the baby is down, the computer comes on, and thousands upon thousands of women seek each other out.

> *Having a baby basically ended all my friendships. I have no time to go out anymore or socialize, but I did end up meeting some great people online.*
>
> —STACEY

Could My Parents Pitch In?

Traditionally, grandparents in the village have played a crucial role in caring for children while younger adults toiled to find, raise, or prepare food. Older adults remain an important part of a child's village, even in a modern world that is vastly different.

Recent census figures show that nearly 5.8 million grandparents live with their grandchildren, and 42 percent are the primary caretakers. The U.S. Census Bureau estimates that the number of children who live in grandparent-headed homes has been rising steadily over the past thirty years.

> *My daughter used to take her baby wherever she goes, no matter how late at night. She's still young, only nineteen, and doesn't understand that's not the way to get a baby good sleep, so when she moved back in, I took over. Now she still goes out, but the baby stays home, and I bathe him and put him to bed at a decent hour.*
>
> —JANICE

When Does Child Care Kick In?

Within weeks or months, many moms are headed back into the work-force. Even if they decide to be stay-at-home moms (known these days as SAHMs), they will need a break once in a while.

When that need arises, day-care providers and after-school program staff become part of the village that raises your child. Reputable day-care centers allow you to drop in without notice, and many have two-way mir-rors to allow you to observe your children without disrupting their play. Some employers offer work-based child-care programs for preschool and after-school, and in most settings, you can find after-school programs for your older children. These programs help bridge that gap between the end of the school day and the time it takes Mom or Dad to get home. Still, the day-care situation in the United States is a patchwork of programs that seldom coordinates well with work and school hours, and you may feel stressed at the time limitations of providers and programs.

> *We registered with a preschool, from 9:00 A.M. to 3:00 P.M.*
> *There is aftercare at the school, though that's not my favorite.*
> *Who designed this? This is ridiculous. It's an outrage. It's a*
> *real a slap at women—I don't even have words to describe*
> *how angry I am at that. In the city, we had day care that went*
> *till six.*
>
> —FAITHE

Those with the financial means may consider hiring a nanny who stays home with the child or children. This can also be a more affordable option for families with young children close in age, since most day-care centers don't offer "bulk" discounts. And while there is a certain stigma of snobbishness attached to having a nanny among those who don't think they can afford one, the payoffs can be more than just financial for a working mom. "Nanny sharing" is also an option that some parents pursue. It cuts costs and provides the flexibility two-income households need.

> *I was worried that I would become resentful when I was alone with a three-year-old and that she would be harmed by that. I know that the nanny's not as fun as me, or as educated or as wacky as me, but ultimately my daughter is happier because seven and a half to nine hours a day, she's with this methodical, measured, solid, structured, careful person. I'm gratified that I'm able to bring a third person to the picture who's going to produce a happier childhood for my daughter.*
>
> —KATE

Can I Call on Neighbors and friends?

If you're combining career and motherhood, having a friend who is a stay-at-home mom can be a lifesaver. Stay-at-home moms (SAHMs) often have the flexibility to pick up two children at once from school—your child and theirs. You can reciprocate by taking the kids on the weekend or a holiday, or a sleepover some night, to give the SAHM a break. Neighbors, especially those with children just a little older than yours, are often willing to help out in a pinch, and a panicked call from the cell phone in the middle of rush-hour traffic is hardly something a good neighbor can ignore.

The parents of your child's friends also become a valuable network for child care, play dates, and emergencies, not to mention a network for your own socializing. As the kids get older, this group becomes invaluable for comparing notes on teachers, coaches, other instructors, interesting events going on around the area, and childrearing hints.

> The first year after my husband died, my mother came a few times. A year later, she died. I felt lost. The neighbors across the way used to have my kids over a lot. I had friends. The kids' friends' parents were nice and welcomed my kids into their homes. I heard one friend talking to my son. "If you ever need a dad, you can have my dad."
>
> —ROSALYN

Much of our life revolved around the small private school our children were attending. It was natural for the parents to have the same interests because of our involvement with this school. To this day, some of these couples are still our best friends. I naturally felt the most comfortable with my friends who had children, since there was so much more to talk about.

—CHRYSTAL

How Can the Schools Help?

Once your child hits kindergarten, life gets a lot easier in many ways. Automatically, there is a place for your child to be from about 8:00 A.M. to about 2:30 P.M., depending on your district. But that doesn't mean teachers are baby-sitters. They play a most important role in a child's life. They are with the children for many of their waking hours and want to talk to parents. They can offer invaluable insights into the growth and well-being of your child.

> *Being a teacher, you see how you know you don't want your child to behave. You see how some kids react to things, and you know that's because that's the way it is at home.*
>
> —ANA

Children with athletic interests are also involved with athletic teachers who can share information about how your child copes with both victory and frustration. Coaches and dance instructors often witness not only a child's physical achievements, but their emotional ones as well. This can become particularly important during the stressful adolescent years, when kids talk to them about issues often too difficult to share with their parents.

Can I Trust What I Read in the Papers?

Many people look to the media for parenting guidance, and the discriminating viewer, listener, and reader can find excellent tips and ideas there. When it gets down to basics, the media are a process for distributing information. It's up to the user to determine its value.

A variety of magazines offer advice on parenting. Some of the biggest and most reputable include *Parenting*, *Child*, *Parents*, and *Working Mother*. When millions of subscribers read the material these magazines offer, the village is affected. Debates about the newest trends from how to teach math to when to spank your child are printed daily, generating a national conversation on how to raise kids right. Television shows ranging from public television to afternoon network talk shows provide a wide (and sometimes scary) variety of parenting experiences, advice, and resources.

And if print and broadcast media aren't enough, there's the Internet. Every day, at all hours of the day and night, people from all over the world jump into chat rooms and onto listservs to discuss their children, their parenting, and their lives. Some of the country's largest Internet service providers have hundreds of chat rooms dedicated to parenting. Parents who look around and see no help can log on and get some advice.

"I don't know what I would do without you guys," said one posting to a popular parenting site. "There's no one around here who understands. But you're all so accepting, and you've got so much wisdom to share. Thank you!"

Online magazines and newsletters also abound. Some of the major ones include NPIN Parent News (http://npin.org/pnews.html), Career-parent.com (careerparent.com), The Successful Parent (thesuccessful parent.com), and SingleParentsMag.com (singleparentsmag.com).

If the Internet isn't your speed or the personal touch is still something you crave, go to your local library. At a decent library, even very young children have a place to explore books and videos. Local library staff can help develop a child's interest in reading by hosting storytelling times to make books fun, treating the children with respect, and giving them the responsibility of a library card.

When Can I Ask for Help?

Pregnant women and young mothers, especially those who are career-driven, independent, and self-confident, will have a hard time ever picking up the phone and asking for help. For most women, this can spell the beginning of disaster, whether it be a nervous breakdown, total exhaustion, or the slow and imperceptible withering away of one's self in the face of other, greater demands.

> *Because health was the biggest factor, I wrote up a sheet for all my coworkers with my meds, hospital visits, times I was supposed to eat, times I was supposed to check my blood sugar, and my exercise schedule. I scheduled maternity leave and made sure that I was as up-to-date on my work as possible when the time got closer. I wanted to be ready for any emergency and I wanted them to be ready as well as to help. They were great!*
>
> —LORETTE

> *I just did what I had to do, minute by minute. I never found time for myself, which is probably why I went wacky. I just did everything all by myself, and then I got a divorce.*
>
> —KATHY

Women who don't mind admitting to others that they are tired, and who ask for help in supervising an energetic toddler, give themselves time to renew their energy and restore their reserves of patience.

Veteran mothers may also need to remind themselves to get some support when they need it. After years of raising children, you may think you've got it all figured out; you can handle it. But your child's adolescence is not a time to muddle through; it's a time for you to be on top of everything your children are doing and all the friends your children have. Knowing when to get help and being able to ask are critical skills in raising children of any age successfully.

Who Will Help with the "Terrible Teens"?

So you decide to become a mother. You wrap your life around your children, and you accept the identity of "Mom" for eternity. Maybe you drop out of the workforce and hang up that career you'd considered, or you cut back to part-time. Maybe you go back into the workforce, only to learn you're miles behind your peers after being out of the loop for five or six years. You gladly accept that loss for the time you got to spend with your children, the hugs, the tears, and the firsts.

Then your kid grows up.

Your teenage children go off into that village to become members themselves. They get jobs, become baby-sitters, have their own friends to see and their own social events to attend. Suddenly, and it will feel sudden, you are not the center of their universe anymore.

To become a mom is to be needed, day in and day out, on call all the time, from the day your baby is born until the day he or she becomes a young adult. As monumental a shift as it may seem to decide on motherhood, the shift that occurs when your children begin to move away, emotionally and physically, can be just as major. And the larger village can play an important—and not always positive—role in the direction your child takes.

> *My kids came of age in the 1970s in a college town, where drugs, sex, and rock and roll ruled the transition from childhood to adulthood. Most kids had ready access to pot and psychedelics through their parents' "hidden" supply. Mine were*

no exception. Underage alcoholism was gaining steam. This
time in our history was radical—radically good, radically
bad—for this batch of kids, and overall it was dysfunctional
for way too many children, mine included.

—STEPHANIE

This is a time for women to call on another part of the village. Mothers of teens will need to look to allies, people like coaches and instructors, possibly the parents of other athletes or friends, who have earned the trust and respect of her children. At this time, a mother will need to rely on them to steer her children in the right direction—and trust that it isn't her fault when the children decide to take a more difficult path. She will also need to seek out appropriate doctors for her children, such as adolescent pediatricians, gynecologists for her girls, family practice doctors, and sometimes mental health professionals.

As her children head off to college or full-time work, she will need to appreciate the entire process of helping them launch their lives. While her young adult will make many, if not all, of those decisions, ultimately she will be the one called upon in a crisis. Letting children go can be even more of a challenge than raising them.

While raising the boys, I missed out on time for myself entirely.
When they were little, I couldn't even go to the bathroom without being interrupted. This crazy being-in-demand thing was
very normal. I try to think of where I'll go from here, now that
they're moving on. I have a friend who goes to a lot of trouble
finding out various shows that are playing, so I can fill up the
time. It's so much easier to take care of other people than take
care of myself.

—HOLLY

The transition from home to away was rocky. When my
daughter graduated from high school, she went to New York
City, but she was overwhelmed. She thought she was going
to be happy, but she was miserable. She came home for six
months, got an apartment, dropped out of school, and then
went to live near her dad. That didn't work out, so she joined

the circus. The worst part of that was that the only contact
I had was when she would call me—usually between acts.

—EVA

That is when moms find one more part of the village to call upon: other empty nesters struggling with the same issues. Often extended family in the same age group are good people to approach. Members of your religious community with children in the same age group also can lend an ear and share a similar story. If your child heads off to college, there will be parents' associations of one sort or another you can join, or perhaps you'll spend this time refocusing on your relationship, your home, and your community.

Where Can I Make Child-free friends?

For women without children, it can seem sometimes like the entire world is made of Disney movies and playgrounds. But there is life without children, and as friends and relatives drop out of your life, you can still actively pursue a fulfilling, well-rounded life with a balance of leisure and work activities and a variety of friends.

> *I've always firmly believed if you're going to have children, their needs have to come before other things in your life. But I really wanted to do other things, careerwise and recreationally. I didn't want my time with those things taken away by children.*
>
> —ELAINE

The Internet, for instance, has expanded by a thousandfold the way people without children can meet, compare notes, rant, commiserate, and celebrate. Childfree.net is one of the most comprehensive websites available for child-free couples. It includes not only links to other websites, but also many useful books and networking groups addressing the needs of singles and couples ranging from child-free by choice to infertile and still grieving.

No Kidding! is an international nonprofit organization that transcends the virtual world by helping people organize local chapters that provide social activities for child-free singles and couples. According to his statement on the website, the founder was tired of justifying his child-free status at social events where everyone assumed he either had children, was going to have children, or was unwell. Chapters exist across the United States and around the world.

> *The first event we went to was Charlie Goodnight's nightclub.*
> *We met two couples there. We now have season tickets to the*
> *Durham Bulls games, because last year we went to a No*
> *Kidding! event there. We take care of each other; we are the*
> *surrogate family. Even when you don't know these people that*
> *well, they're very embracive.*
>
> —ROBYN

Infertility support groups are available for women who can't conceive without medical intervention or decide not to pursue it. You will find support groups among infertile women. RESOLVE is the nation's largest organization dedicated to issues of infertility, but there are others, including the American Infertility Association. Your doctor may also know of some local ones you can contact.

Sports and active-lifestyle groups are another option for child-free women inundated by a variety of community-based activities that are focused on children. Active-lifestyle magazines and websites can tweak your imagination in new ways, giving you ideas for child-free activities you haven't considered since you were a child yourself.

> *I like the ability to go places when I want to and not worry*
> *about what am I going to do with the children.*
>
> —LAURICE

> *I've been able to do all kinds of other things—been able to take*
> *classes, do a lot of writing, taken vacations by myself.*
>
> —SUZIE

One woman volunteered to clean up the beach of the local lake one weekend a month each summer, and another spearheaded an all-woman Habitat for Humanity construction project. You may find yourself in a mixed group of young people and older adults whose children are grown, but that only expands your network of friends and experiences.

Just because you decide not to have your own children, it doesn't mean you don't like to spend time with children. Nationally and locally, there are hundreds of organizations that work with children, the elderly, homeless people, people with disabilities, people fighting for economic and social justice, or even just other folks who like to cook. They are always looking for volunteers. Moms you know are often looking for a break from their kids and would welcome an offer to take the kids for an afternoon or a sleepover. Most mothers wouldn't think to impose on a woman without children, so it's up to you to make the call. It can be a nice break for Mom and a good time for you to enjoy a "rent-a-kid."

> *When I go to temple, I just put a kid on my lap. We do this a lot; we pass babies around. We call them temple babies. I'll chat people up. "Ever want to go out to dinner by yourself? We can take the baby." We do a lot of Saturday nights. People leave their kids off, and they can go out for a while, and I become friendly with people I might not have been friendly with. Sometimes I'm kind of surprised.*
>
> —MYRA

You can also become a Big Sister, Girl Scout leader, or volunteer at the local school or library if you want to spend more time with children. While it may take more motivation and imagination to find this village, it is out there, and in many respects, it is growing.

8

How Will Children Affect My Career?

Until now, it has been taboo, except for a brief moment during the surge of the women's movement in the seventies, to compare the personal growth from a career or other pursuit to the personal growth that motherhood provides us. Who dared to say the miracle of childbirth and the unconditional love of a child belongs in the same category with anything else life has to offer? But times appear to be changing, with more U.S. women than ever before opting not to have children (19 percent in 2000, compared with 10 percent in 1976). Our interviews, surveys, and research show that while many women appreciate the miracle of childbirth and childrearing, they also appreciate the huge sacrifices that women make in order to be mothers—and they are not always willing to make them.

What if I Don't Want to Give Up My Career?

College-age women approach their upcoming work lives by planning to "balance career and family." As they mature, however, many career women find those plans altered by time and circumstances. For example, Sylvia Hewlett, author of *Creating a Life*, documented that almost 50 percent of the high-powered women she surveyed did not have children. She also recounts a profound sense of loss some of these women described concerning their childlessness as they got older.

It is also true, however, that it is much easier to pine for the option you didn't choose. For example, career women in their early thirties often report feeling envy as they watch satisfied-looking stay-at-home moms interacting with their infants and toddlers. At the same time, women who focused first on motherhood report a sense of sadness watching women in business attire chatting over lunch.

If you are used to heading off into the fast pace of the business world, you may discover that you are bored to tears with an infant. In those six to eight weeks before newborns will even let you know that they know you exist, a highly energetic, Type A woman may feel like she's on a leash tied to her home, hardly able to accomplish anything between baby's naps, the sudden increase in home chores, and her own exhaustion.

> *There is definitely increased stress. I can never just go do what I want without making arrangements for my children. I always have to work around them.*
>
> —DEBBIE

Working mothers face the stress of their guilt at leaving their child in someone else's hands, the difficulty of finding good, reliable, and affordable child care, the rush to be home to be on time for day care or a nanny, the responsibility of getting baby and baby's food ready before work in the morning, new tasks like making play dates, and more. A supportive and active partner lightens the load, of course. Still, in most households today, this work falls on Mom.

> It's been challenging arranging play dates. It's caused me to
> have to be significantly more proactive and outgoing than I
> normally would have been. My husband says, "I'd do this if
> I could," but we all know it's the women who do this. People
> might think he's some kind of weird letch, crazy guy if he
> called up and asked Suzie's mom if she'd like to meet at the
> park for a play date.
>
> —NEVA

> I went back to work because after three months of staying
> home with my child, I was going bonkers. I couldn't stand
> staying home with a baby all day—I had to get out of the
> house. And my husband wouldn't give me any money; I
> had to ask. So I needed my own money.
>
> —JERI

Of course, you must decide for yourself what represents the best balance of work, relationships, family, and personal pursuits. You can create a life that allows for your own development as a person, aside from—or in addition to—your many other roles. And the decision to remain child-free still has a greater impact on women's careers than on men's.

> It's a really good thing I didn't have children because they'd
> just be in the way. It's a decision that evolved over time, as I
> was revising my life goals and career goals, figuring out what I
> really wanted to do when I grew up and realizing that children
> didn't fit into that plan.
>
> —IRENE

It wasn't the way I expected. It was hard going back to work after such a long time away. I found I didn't remember some stuff, and other stuff had changed. Everyone expected me to just know everything. It's also hard to concentrate on work when you are thinking about your kid or kids.

—TRINI

Could I Turn into a SAHM?

Some women who were once career-oriented are surprised at how strongly they feel inclined to stay home with their baby.

> *I used to be very ambitious. That's not to say I have no ambition now, but I have gone from wanting to be the best in my area and living for promotions to being quite happy to be where I'm at in my job. It is a choice I couldn't have imagined making eight years ago.*
>
> —CARI

> *I was surprised how little I wanted to go back to work after my son was born. I had expected to get sick of his crying and "babyness" quite quickly, but instead, I couldn't bear to leave him at all. My career seemed meaningless; for the first time in my life, it was "just a job."*
>
> —CHRISTINE

If you decide to leave your career completely, then you face a new household landscape: you become dependent on your partner's paycheck, which can cause your sense of independence to stagger. You become a stay-at-home mom (SAHM) and wonder what lies ahead in your new role. You may worry about the career you left behind. What if something happens to your partner, for instance? And at times—however briefly—you may resent this little being you've brought into the world for "holding you back."

But many women never look back at their work lives. They discover that motherhood is quite comfortable and that, except for a rough day here or there with a colicky baby, they can master it very effectively.

> *I could never finish anything that I started at home. I didn't realize how much of an intrusion it would become as I devoted all my time to my three sons. I was tired more than once, but I still tried and became "Supermom," or should I say "Super Earth Mother."*
>
> —EILEEN

Can I Take Time Off for a While to Have Kids?

For most younger, college-educated women, your primary focus is your career goal, be it starting a practice, climbing the corporate ladder, or otherwise establishing yourself as a professional. If you are headed for an executive or professional position, you may want to know that Sylvia Ann Hewlett's survey of women executives showed that only 16 percent of high-achieving women thought you can "have it all" with both career and family. That gives having both work and family, under current policy and economic conditions, a pretty slim chance of success—except under extremely favorable circumstances.

> *I would have been a brilliant and happier mom if I had had a number of servants. And not any old servants. I'm thinking of the caliber of servant Madonna has in her employ. These are very expensive and you have to treat them even better than you treat the children, because they are helping to care for the children—your children. Better yet, hire a village. Make sure the cooks like to cook and the floor washers like to wash floors, or are so highly paid they sing while they wash.*
>
> —SHAR

To make it manageable, many women consider the option of *sequencing*—a term used for women who drop out of the workforce long enough to have children, get their children off to a good start, and then reenter the workforce.

*I have my career on hold right now to stay home. I am a nurse,
so I should be able to get a job any time if need be by staying
up on my credentials.*

—CLARA

*I dropped out of college before I had our first. I was fortunate
to find a series of jobs that I like that paid decently . . . I just
completed my master's and am now devoting much more time
to doing the work I was trained for . . . I am so grateful to have
both aspects of life—parenting and a career—sequentially.*

—FAYE

Of course, in many professions, women (and men) suffer a penalty for walking away for a few years. Even if you have kept up your skills and you return to the same occupation, it is likely that you won't be in the same place as your peers who never left. In the meantime, personal and business relationships have grown cold and the profession's collective memory of your reputation for hard work, creativity, or charisma has faded. Your peers, who have "paid their dues" all along, may well be next in line for the promotion you might have had coming to you if you'd stayed.

*Looking back, I thought that working at home would keep my
fingers in the professional pie. But when my husband left and I
did have to find a job to support myself, I learned that I had to
start over with an entry-level job and jump to an appropriate
professional level five years later.*

—STELLA

A support group and advice on this approach to work and family is available at mothersandmore.com. You can also read more background, though a bit dated, in the book *Sequencing: A New Solution for Women Who Want Marriage, Career, and Family,* by Arlene Rossen Cardozo.

Where Are the Kid-Friendly Careers?

Career-oriented women who want to "have it all" find several careers especially kid-friendly, either for their shorter or more flexible hours or for their flexible work location. These careers include teaching, other school employment, freelance writing or consulting, graphic design, any kind of telecommuting or Internet-based work, and social work. Remember, though, that with self-employment, you have to provide your own paid vacation and retirement fund. You'll have to fend for yourself, often while also keeping your toddler out of the fine china as you discuss the latest project with your client.

> *I had to cut back on regular hours, since I am the primary caretaker. I have branched out into writing reasonably successfully, but my family has no sense of deadlines!*
>
> —VAL

> *Since I'm self-employed, there hasn't been much impact on my career. I didn't tell a few of my clients that I was pregnant, or that I had a new baby, or that I have a neurotic border collie and I'm painting the house. As long as I meet deadlines and do great work, they will hire me again.*
>
> —SHARON

*I feel like my daughter comes first, so I work twenty hours a
week now, and I have two home businesses to take up the slack
and still be with her as much as possible.*

—MARGIE

Experiences in other countries show that if you work in a field that
provides flexible hours, family-friendly policies, and the option of part-
time work while raising young children, you are more likely to succeed
at both career and family. Various leading feminists (and others) over the
last twenty years have advocated the specifics of these policies, including Sylvia Ann Hewlett, Gloria Steinem, Robin Morgan, Felice Schwartz
(who sparked the original firestorm over the "mommy track" in the
1980s), and Arlene Rossen Cardozo, the author of *Sequencing*. Some
options include flexible schedules, paid parental leave, disability benefits
for pregnancy (federal law currently requires that pregnancy-related disabilities be treated the same as other disabilities), worksite child-care
facilities, and generous family health insurance coverage. Every year,
Working Mother magazine prints its rankings of employers offering such
family-friendly benefits; other magazines rank employers as well. No matter whether she is interviewing with a company that has made it onto
such a list, a woman should discuss these issues one-on-one with a prospective employer to make sure those practices are in place.

Current U.S. policy still doesn't favor families. Here are some ideas of
what to look for in a family-friendly employer:

- Flexible work schedules
- Sick leave and vacation pools
- Carryover of vacation and sick leave from year to year
- Day care on-site or nearby
- Paid family health insurance
- Tuition assistance for children of employees
- Job categories that don't require night and weekend work or signifi-
  cant out-of-town travel
- Unpaid leave with guaranteed return to similar job

I didn't really derail my career; I just changed it. I got off partner track and got this new title "of counsel," and I reduced my hourly commitment to thirty hours a week. I got off the radar screen you're on at a big firm—that horrible monster of billable hours you have to feed every day. Now instead of a monster, it's more like a Saint Bernard in the back of my station wagon.

—YVONNE

Of course, childrearing doesn't have to fall only on the woman. These days, couples have been very imaginative about keeping a parent at home with the children. Some couples elect to have Mom keep working while Dad stays home.

When my husband decided to take time off, I said, "I'm going to go for it. I'm going to concentrate on my job." I work really hard. I work long hours. I am thankful that I ended up with my husband because he is an enlightened man, and that's why I chose him. I didn't choose him for his earning power.

—MARJORIE

9

What Does It Cost to Have and Raise Children?

Plenty of people will tell you that having and raising children is an expensive proposition, but seldom does anyone actually do the math. And for many women, there is no reason to. Knowing that children are expensive isn't likely to be relevant if you've already made up your mind to have kids. But if you haven't decided or would like to plan ahead, it may help to know what the financial challenges are likely to be.

What Do Fertility Treatments Cost?

If you discover you are having trouble conceiving and you want technological assistance, you should contact a fertility expert, generally a gynecologist specializing in reproductive endocrinology. The single factor that best predicts your chances of success with any advanced fertility treatment is the age of your eggs. (They are all present at your birth, so the age of the eggs is the same as your age.)

There are different levels of fertility treatment, with new technologies published almost monthly in specialized medical journals. The best-known and most commonly used is in vitro fertilization (IVF), referred to in previous decades as creating "test tube babies" due to the fact that the eggs are fertilized in highly specialized labs before being implanted in a woman's uterus. Research suggests that a woman's chances of achieving a birth following IVF are typically 20 to 50 percent depending on her age, health, and other circumstances.

IVF costs between $10,000 and $15,000 each time you go through an attempted fertilization/implantation cycle. Some insurance plans cover fertility treatments up to a stated maximum, but others offer no coverage at all.

We were using his money, and I was very conscious, but to do the whole in vitro process with one egg was a huge risk and likely to fail. I was essentially asking him to take $15,000 and *flush it down the toilet. He was very understanding. He said, "Let me get this right—this is the only egg we have and might be the only egg we'll ever have?" I just told him, "Oh, I love you so much."*

—RHONDA

After two cycles we had to decide: take another chance on IVF or take what money we had left and put it into pursuing adoption. We hated having to base our decision on finances, and there were no guarantees either way. It was so hard.

—MARSHA

What Does Artificial Insemination Cost?

If your male partner has fertility problems (which is the case in 40 percent of infertile couples), if you are single, or if you and your lesbian partner want a child, you may opt for artificial insemination. This option will result in a baby with a genetic connection to you and to a sperm donor, who is usually anonymous. Artificial insemination is relatively inexpensive. Sperm banks charge between $300 and $800 for a supply of sperm and will hold more samples (for a fee) in case the couple or woman wants more children with the same genetic connection. Upscale sperm banks now offer not only descriptions of the physical characteristics of donors, including their medical history and family history, but genetic consultations and childhood photos or audio interviews with the donor.

> I made the decision to do artificial insemination because it was sort of financial. It's very expensive to adopt—at least $10,000—whereas if I tried to get pregnant (I wouldn't go the route of IVF or hormone therapy), I was just going to try insemination, and that was not exorbitantly priced.
>
> —ANGIE

What Does It Cost to Have a Baby?

Most doctors and midwives roll their fees into a total cost for prenatal care, labor, and delivery. Many charge the same fee for a vaginal or cesarean delivery. Insurance is likely to cover some of this fee, which averages about $2,400.

The cost for routine office visits is usually built into the prenatal package of services offered by the physician for helping you have your baby. If your pregnancy gets complicated, the charges for extra medical testing or visits with consulting physicians will be add-ons.

Moms over thirty-five and moms with blood-screening tests that suggest fetal anomalies will usually be offered amniocentesis, to rule out genetic abnormalities. The charge for the procedure itself will be separate from the charge for genetic testing and counseling. These charges historically have been poorly compensated by third-party payers.

Moms of all ages with chronic conditions like diabetes and hypertension will probably incur additional charges for lab tests, additional ultrasounds, and nonstress testing. All the additional testing is directed toward making your baby as healthy as possible at delivery. Insurance coverage is variable but usually better than for genetic testing.

Many women elect to get their prenatal care through midwifery services. Midwives can provide most pregnancy care and can be an important addition to the care you receive in the hospital. Because they can't perform emergency surgery and often do not have the training, facilities, or equipment to handle major complications, many midwives have professional relationships with medical doctors in the area. If you develop complications during pregnancy or delivery, you will pay midwife fees above and beyond the cost of any medical intervention by the supervising doctor and/or health care institution.

Hospital costs for labor and delivery averaged $5,226 in 1998, according to industry expert HCIA-Sachs. The average cost of a cesarean delivery was $12,020. Charges that remain your responsibility beyond what your health insurance pays vary from plan to plan.

Many women choose freestanding birthing centers with the hope and expectation that they will receive more personalized care and have more control over the birthing process. These centers estimate that they can reduce labor and delivery costs by 30 to 50 percent because of lower overhead and fewer medical interventions.

For reasons not always related to cost, the appeal of at-home births is spreading. It's a setting we don't recommend. If a pregnant woman or her infant is in distress, the amount of time it takes to get her to the hospital can mean the difference between joy and tragedy.

Finally, if your pregnancy gets so complicated that you have to stop work to be on bed rest, you'll need to factor the loss of your income into the total expense of having the baby.

What Will It Take to Outfit the Baby's Room?

While baby's homecoming can be the most daunting of times, a young couple can tap into a number of resources to help ease the financial pain of outfitting the baby's room.

Essentials for the new baby obviously include diapers, T-shirts, sleepwear, a crib and/or bassinet, a baby carrier/car seat (often made in combination these days), and probably a stroller. There are a number of good websites that can help you calculate the costs of these and other items. (Parenting.com has one of the best.)

Our culture, like many others, has a built-in ritual for helping young parents contend with the expense of a new baby. It's called the baby shower. Expectant mothers should be very clear about the assistance they need, because their friends want to supply them with gifts they'll find most useful.

There's yet another cultural tradition, usually reserved for closer friends, called hand-me-downs. New moms often acquire a treasure trove of nearly new clothes and toys from in-laws, neighbors, and friends who know that their own baby used them only a month or two before growing out of them. Often, veteran moms are glad to get the goods out of their attics and closets, and you'll be relieved to have a full nursery without emptying your wallet.

Of course, many of these supplies will be used again by baby number two if you choose to have another, so the expense of these items decreases after your first child. On the other hand, if you're surprised to discover you're having twins, you face exceptional additional costs. Assume your costs will double, and be grateful when you find more than one friend who has an old crib or storage bag full of baby clothes you can use.

> *At the beginning, we spent way too much on "things" we were sure the baby needed. As time went on, we realized she could have used clothes from the consignment store, and she really didn't have to have every Elmo toy that hit the market, as soon as it hit the market. We continued to pay top dollar for diapers—we never could buy into the bargain brands. And because I delivered early, my milk never really came in, so we had to buy fairly expensive preemie formula for quite some time.*
>
> —EDIE

For safety reasons, there are some items you will probably not want to skimp on or pick up secondhand. These include older cribs (which may have bars that a baby can push his head through), earlier generations of car seats (which may not meet current safety standards), or certain wind-up swings and other items that have been recalled. Information and updates on safety standards and recalls can be found on the Web at safetyforum.com, which also has discussion forums and a search mechanism so you can look up a particular product.

What Does It Cost to Raise a Child?

American families making over $65,800 per year will spend almost $338,000 to raise a child born in 2001 through age seventeen. Families earning between $39,100 and $65,800 will spend about $231,500, and lower-income families, those making less than $39,100, will spend $170,000. These figures from the U.S. Department of Agriculture don't include an estimated $40,000 to $150,000 for a four-year college education. (The USDA, which has been providing such estimates since 1960, publishes this annual report through its Center for Nutrition Policy and Promotion.)

That means raising one child costs about $14,000 per year for a family making over $65,000, a second child runs that bill up to $19,000, and a third to more than $22,000. Taking into account all income ranges, the average cost of raising a child ranges from $7,000 to $14,000 per year. Geographically, it is most expensive to raise children in the urban West, with the urban Northeast coming in second, and the urban Midwest and rural areas being the least expensive. These figures don't include exceptional expenses such as private school or costs related to disabilities.

Raising a child as a single mom is more difficult than doing it on two incomes. (Most single-parent families fall into the lower-income category, so a larger portion of their total income is spent raising children.) Expenses vary radically depending not only on what part of the country you live in, but on whether you choose an urban, suburban, or rural area. If you take a hiatus from building your career, it will affect your income and your retirement. And if you have a career that allows for a genuine "mommy track," you may compare less favorably in position and salary with your colleagues.

How is this expensive pie sliced? Housing represents the biggest single expense of raising children, eating up between 33 and 37 percent of the annual bill. The USDA assumes that for each child you have, you will add 100 to 150 square feet of living space to your home.

Feeding your children is the second largest expense, accounting for 15 to 20 percent of your total annual cost. Cars, gas, repairs, and public transportation can add up to between 13 and 14 percent of the total expense of having children. Child care averages 10 percent of the overall annual expense of raising children, with the highest costs coming between the ages of three and five. The Children's Defense Fund estimates that the average is $4,210 for full-time care of a three-year-old. But national averages don't tell the whole story. In major metropolitan areas, for instance, these costs will be significantly higher. Child Care Aware and the Nanny Network are two organizations that will help you estimate your costs based on your local economy—see the Resources. The federal government offers a child-care tax credit, but the cost can still be an immense and surprising burden, even in affluent households.

Additionally, clothing can run between 6 and 8 percent of your total costs. Miscellaneous expenses like personal care items, entertainment, and reading materials take up a total of 10 to 13 percent of the total cost of raising a child.

Health care makes up about 7 percent of the total annual cost. These expenses include medical and dental expenses not covered by insurance, as well as insurance premiums not paid by an employer or other organization. These expenses increase exponentially if your child has disabilities or a chronic illness.

It's difficult to imagine other expenses before you actually have children. Some surprises: the increased cost of vacations, such as the extra plane ticket or extra hotel room, and gifts for birthday parties and for holidays. If your child shows an interest in music or dance, then add the cost of lessons throughout the years. Athletes now pay extra fees for uniforms in most school districts. And one of the newer expenses for parents is computers. With rapid changes in technology, parents can expect to purchase several computers for each child during the first seventeen years, then likely another one for college.

More optional expenses include private school, which can run as high as college tuition and expenses, and in-home child care, which can range from about $300 per week to several thousand dollars per month.

> *The sitter's going to pull ahead of you for a while—more than half of your net pay. Is it worth it to work? I thought at some point about doing child care at home, but I'm just not good being at home 24/7.*
>
> —LOIS

What Will Education Cost?

College is expensive and getting more expensive all the time. If you save at the rate of $140 per month at 5 percent interest, you should be able to pay for one child to go to a public four-year college ($45,000) eighteen years from now. This is assuming, of course, that tuition rises at only 8 percent annually, as it did until recently. In the last two years, some public universities have seen tuition jumps of 20 percent or more each year.

If you save at the rate of $600 per month at 5 percent interest, you should be able to pay for one child to attend private college ($205,000) eighteen years from now. Again, this is conservative, based on an 8 percent per year tuition increase. These figures only predict tuition and living expenses. They do not include travel home for holidays, your travel to university events in distant cities, health insurance, car insurance, or a host of other expenses too long to list.

> We thought we had her college savings set, but then the stock market took a dive a couple of years ago, and suddenly she's a senior in high school, and we're struggling with what to do the next year. We had to make some tough choices, but she's in college and working, and she's applied for some loans. It'll work.
>
> —TANYA

What Price Will I Pay for Not Working?

Many women are choosing to take time off from their careers to get their children off to a good start. When they return to work, they may find that others who have stayed in the game are far ahead of where they are. A subset of these women will change their career into one more conducive to being home more to be with the kids.

Some research shows that many women aren't interested in returning to full-time work once they've spent time at home with their children. Arlene Rossen Cardozo, author of the book *Sequencing: A New Solution for Women Who Want Marriage, Career, and Family*, writes that 90 percent of the working mothers she spoke to sought part-time work and flexible schedules to accommodate their desire to spend more time with their children. While she puts a positive spin on a woman's chances of returning to work at the same level at which she left, Cardozo also makes it clear that women have made new demands on employers, and that at least some employers are responding favorably.

As we noted before, some women never return to work, often surprised at their pleasure of becoming full-time moms or inhibited by the notion of balancing work and family. In her bestselling book, *The Price of Motherhood*, Ann Crittenden documents the price of substituting full-time motherhood for a full-time career. She cites economist Shirley Burggraf, who has calculated the loss of income in a two-parent family in which one equal wage earner drops out of the workforce. A couple with a combined income of $81,500 stands to lose $1.35 million in that scenario, most of it through lost wages. A middle-income family in which one partner makes $30,000 and the other averages $15,000 stands to lose more than $600,000. Referring to this as the "mommy tax," Crittenden makes a compelling argument for social and governmental changes we need to neutralize economic discrimination against families.

Women who return to work with no reduction in their work schedule are still coming up against a prejudice most thought no longer existed. Between 1981 and 1990, wages of women without children rose from 72 to 90 percent of men's wages, but working mothers' wages rose only from 60 percent to 70 percent of men's wages in that same decade. Stereotypes aside, it is still true that working mothers are less likely to be available for impromptu late-night meetings, extensive travel, or unscheduled overtime, making it harder for them to compete with child-free coworkers or men with stay-at-home wives. In addition, the cost (and time) of raising children may inhibit a mom, working or not, from furthering her education and increasing her earning potential for later in life. Yet, surprisingly, a recent national survey shows that working mothers actually average more hours per week on the job than their child-free counterparts.

> *Having kids affected the financial side of my going back to school. I wanted to go back to graduate school, and I said, "Let's talk about money." There just wasn't that money to do it.*
>
> —SAMANTHA

> *It's a lot to juggle—working and the kids and the husband. I usually feel like I can't give a hundred percent to any one thing in my life, but I don't want to give any of it up.*
>
> —GRETCHEN

> *I love my kids and would die for them without hesitation, but when they arrived, I lost many of the things I loved to do. I have had to cut back drastically on my work and my hobbies, which is hard.*
>
> —CATHY

In addition, women are not yet compensated for the work they do at home. If they were compensated, conservative and somewhat dated estimates have them worth more than $60,000 per year. That's lost income. For a mom working outside the home, it's a paycheck she'll never see for that second shift at home. For a stay-at-home mom, that's also a paycheck she'll never see, on top of the income she's losing by not being in the workforce. Either way, it's a big hit on an economic level.

A number of websites allow you to calculate the cost of having a child using numbers more specific to your circumstances. If this is an aspect of motherhood that you find important, we encourage you to check out the sites we have listed and read some of the books on the market that speak to the issue.

How Would I Cope with the Cost of a Disability?

More than five million American children between the ages of three and twenty-one have disabilities. Disabilities range from those present at birth to physical, emotional, and learning disorders not recognized until later in childhood.

If you bear a child with disabilities or your child develops a problem, finding a way to finance the special needs of that child can be very challenging. You may encounter the expenses of multiple hospitalizations, frequent doctor's visits, travel to clinics specializing in the disability (including hotel stays for the parents), obscure procedures not covered by insurance, purchase or rental of at-home medical equipment, and in the long run, financial arrangements for the long-term care of your child after your death.

Financial assistance and some legal protection is available for these children, but parents of children with disabilities will tell you it's never enough. School districts, for instance, are required by law to provide facilities and education tailored to the special needs of your disabled child. Federal assistance is available through Social Security and other public assistance sources. Unfortunately, this assistance can fluctuate with political trends and budget priorities, so it is difficult to rely on it over time. You can also set up special-needs trusts to ensure a financially secure future for your children. It's a rough road, emotionally and financially, for any parent, but parents of special-needs children often say they found reserves of inner strength and imaginative financial solutions they never would have dreamed of so that their children could receive proper care.

I stayed off work for four years to take care of my daughter. My ex-husband was paying some child support, my parents helped, and I got Social Security Disability Insurance from the government. My employer cobbled two part-time jobs together to make a full-time job so I could get benefits. They've been great at my job.

—IRENE

10

What if I Change My Mind?

By now there can be no doubt that, for many women, the decision to become a mother is fraught with ambivalence. Throughout our childhood, into our teen years, sometimes well into our twenties and thirties, the see-saw of motherhood versus a life without children bounces up and down in the back of our minds.

Sometimes we decide to live the child-free life through our best reproductive years, then decide we want children, only to discover that pregnancy doesn't come easily or at all. At other times, the Fates force us to confront it rather suddenly, with an unintended pregnancy.

Can I Have Kids After Forty?

Assisted reproductive technology (ART) is still a young field, rife with difficulty, offering no guarantees, and often disappointing many anxious, desperate couples. Even so, ART has been able to fulfill the dreams of many couples who otherwise would never have had children of their own.

In 1999, just over 30,000 babies resulted from almost 87,000 cycles of ART. Some of these were multiple births, making the odds per individual woman lower than they appear. The actual number of term pregnancies (of one or *more* living infants) is closer to 21,500 out of 87,000. At least one critic within the field, Dr. Joseph Schulman, believes that even these numbers are high. Clinics are required by law to publish their live-birth rate, so Schulman sees an incentive for clinics to choose younger women, or women in better health, which makes their numbers look better and brings in more prospective patients.

Fertility clinics are available in every major city and most university towns. Women in rural areas will most likely have to travel for advanced fertility services. The best place to find a directory of fertility clinics is on the Internet; type "fertility clinics" or "infertility clinics" into any search engine. Besides searching online, you can find directories of fertility clinics by calling or visiting major libraries and requesting help from a research librarian.

If you discover that your own eggs are not sufficient for fertilization, you may decide to consider egg donation. This process is considerably more complex than sperm donation. You will have to factor in the additional cost of the donor and consider the fact that your child, if you have one, will not have your genetic makeup.

I tried for seven years with my own eggs, and I was so depressed. It didn't make sense to try again, and we certainly couldn't afford an egg donor. I opened up to a girlfriend about the problem, and she said, "I've got eggs. You can have some of mine." We still had to take out a second mortgage on the house, but she went through two cycles for us. I couldn't believe it.

—MARYBETH

Can I Adopt Late in Life?

The demand to adopt healthy infants has steadily increased since the end of World War II. The latest U.S. figures showed about a half million people were seeking to adopt a child, with only 100,000 having actually applied. There are about 3.3 adoption seekers for every adoption.

Most adoptive families are two-parent families in which the parents are between the ages of thirty-one and forty. There is a slightly increasing trend toward adoption by older couples. Most adoptive parents have attended college or completed a college degree, and those participating in independent (private) adoptions tend to be in a higher income bracket than those adopting through public agencies.

Higher rates of adoption applications are seen among women who wanted three or more children, women who have suffered fetal loss or the death of a child, women who were or had been married, and women who were older. African-American women were as likely to seek adoption as women of other races, and more single men than ever are adopting.

Single-parent adoption is steadily increasing in both domestic and international adoptions. The majority of these adoptions are by single women who adopt older children they have cared for as foster parents. Prospective single parents have a tougher time adopting a child, even though numerous studies show that single-parent adoptions have outcomes that are no different or are better for the adopted children. Single parents make many more attempts at adoption before getting a child than couples of similar ages and means. Single-parent domestic adoptions also include higher rates of "hard to place" children (minority, mixed ancestry, disabled, or older).

Laws passed in 1994 and 1996 prohibit the practice of basing adoptions on the race, color, or national origin of the adoptive or foster parent or the child involved. The most recent adoption figures show that less than 10 percent of adoptions are transracial, but 15 percent of all foster child adoptions are transracial. One percent of white women adopt black children, 5 percent of white women adopt children of other races, and 2 percent of women of other races adopt white children, including foreign-born children.

These days, public agencies almost exclusively process adoptions of children with special needs. These are the least expensive option for parents, costing from nearly nothing to about $2,500, including travel and attorney's fees. Most states, under a federal match program, will reimburse nonrecurring adoption expenses up to a set limit. Women and couples interested in pursuing public agency adoptions can get support from the government by contacting organizations that specialize in the area.

Private agencies may charge up to an estimated $30,000 or more. This includes the costs for birth-parent counseling, adoptive parent home study and preparation, child's birth expenses, postplacement supervision until the adoption is finalized, and a portion of agency costs for overhead and operating expenses. Legal fees can run into the thousands of dollars as well.

Independent adoption, where prospective parents use an adoption attorney and may advertise in newspapers and on the Internet seeking a birth mother willing to give up her child, also can run in excess of $30,000 (although some lawyers estimate much less), depending on how much the parents advertise and how many birth-mother expenses they pay. Those expenses won't be repaid, even if the birth mother changes her mind. In some states, the adoptive parents must pay not only their own legal expenses but also those of the birth mother, and some states regulate exactly which expenses the prospective parents must pay.

> We had many failed attempts at adoption in this country. At least three times, when the baby was going to be in my arms, I could practically feel her, it fell through. We went through a lot of savings supporting birth mothers who fell off the planet after the baby came.
>
> —KELLIE

What About International Adoption?

One advantage of many international adoptions is the age factor. Unlike most American adoption agencies, countries such as China consider older parents a more desirable fit for babies. But parents who adopt internationally face a challenge that is rare in domestic adoptions: assimilating their child into the adoptive culture and community while maintaining the child's awareness of his or her birth culture.

Parents of children adopted from other countries also have the challenge of limited access to the child's medical history. Many children have been abandoned, or the agencies in the country of origin don't keep or forward such records. Parents considering international adoption should know that there is almost no way to hedge the risk of adopting a child who will develop special needs. The U.S. State Department does require an independent medical examination by a U.S physician, but even this can't identify medical conditions that may develop over time. For instance, children awaiting adoption may get very limited stimulation or individual attention, which puts them at high risk for developmental delays and later psychological difficulty. In war-torn or AIDS-ravaged countries, some children may be exposed to unimaginable horrors, which can also have a lasting effect on their emotional development.

International private-agency or independent adoption is estimated to cost $7,000 to $25,000 or more. These costs include agency fees, immigration processing fees, and court costs. International adoptions are rife with additional expenses, including child foster care, parents' travel, and escorting fees. Some countries also charge the cost of the child's health care. But as we've mentioned before, older adoptive parents may be operating under better financial circumstances, and the expense is secondary to other issues surrounding the adoption.

> *When it became clear China adoption was a certainty and we just had to get through the paperwork, I played devil's advocate with my husband: When she's this age, we'll be that age, and we won't be around when she's married. I looked at what my sister had done with her kids and asked, "Do I want to go roller-skating and backpacking?" I had serious doubts about that. But when he started to reverse positions, I started to panic. Having our daughter in our lives has healed me. I don't feel any regret for not having a biological child. I never thought I could say that. She's completely changed that for me. I just wish I were thirty-five.*
>
> —HEATHER

Can I Terminate This Pregnancy?

Because of very serious time constraints on the abortion decision, women who want to terminate an unwanted or mistimed pregnancy must act quickly to find an abortion provider. (Women can find the abortion provider nearest them online at the National Abortion Federation: pro choice.org.) Rural women who need abortions may have to travel to a major city or across state lines in order to terminate their pregnancy. Doctors who provide abortion services risk their lives every day to provide this service, sometimes wearing bulletproof vests to and from work. Some clinics may have long lists of women awaiting the procedure and must do a careful juggling act to get all of them in before it's too late to perform the procedure legally. Still, once a woman finds a clinic, she will walk into a supportive, confidential environment where she will receive counseling that explains all of her choices before she goes forward with her decision.

> *By the time I got to the clinic, I knew I wanted an abortion, but the counselor there made me sit down and think it all through one more time. That was very helpful, and it helped me be sure I was making the right decision. It made a big difference in my outlook. I don't feel like I did it in a panic now. I have no regrets.*
>
> —TAMMY

Warning: clinics that use the words "crisis pregnancy" in their advertising and any listings under "abortion alternatives" in the phone book or on the Internet do not consider abortion an option. These "clinics" will claim to offer free services such as counseling, but the staff may offer vague answers when you ask about who will help with the cost of labor and delivery or adoption. As for the "counseling" they provide, women's health clinic staff report hearing often from women who received terrifying misinformation—for example, that they would get cut open, that they wouldn't be able to have babies after an abortion, or that there is a link between abortion and breast cancer (which recently has been refuted once again by scientific evidence).

If you find yourself in one of these "clinics" by accident, don't feel bad; it happens to a lot of women. Just say thank you and leave. For legitimate abortion clinics, contact the National Abortion Federation, the Association of Reproductive Health Professionals, or Planned Parenthood Federation. For adoption, contact a legitimate adoption attorney or agency for assistance. (See the Resources.)

Can I Put This Baby Up for Adoption?

Less than 3 percent of unmarried white women and 2 percent of African-American women put their children up for adoption. Those who do so voluntarily usually come from higher socioeconomic backgrounds, have more education, and come from intact families that support them in their decision.

Women who choose to have their baby and put it up for adoption have many helpful resources at their disposal. If their baby is expected to be healthy, many women can find couples eager to adopt who will pay their medical expenses during pregnancy. The pregnant woman still retains all rights to the baby until she signs the final documents after the birth, so she risks nothing.

11

Will I Be a Good Mom?

There is no way to know if you'll be a good mom until you have a child, but it may help you to consciously define for yourself what a "good mom" is. Every day we face societal images, expectations, and idealizations of motherhood. Contrary to those idealized images, however, all mothers are human. They face the same trials and tribulations, cry at the same disappointments, and scream into their pillow at the same frustrations that the rest of us do.

What if I fail?

The *fear* of failure is real for women considering motherhood, but actual failure is much less common. It's true you won't be optimal every moment, but being an honestly imperfect parent gives you more latitude than trying to be perfect. The added bonus is that children are very forgiving.

> It's stress and strain and a lot of work to have kids, but they give you lots of chances to do it right.
>
> —CARRIE

> I've realized that in parenting, there is no "failure," meaning you're never "out." You fail every day, and you win every day, and you still have to do it the next day. You can't just give up and go home. There is no giving up.
>
> —EILEEN

For some women, fears about motherhood begin to surface after they become pregnant and as they realize a baby is really coming—usually with the first ultrasound where they can actually identify the fetus, when the pregnancy starts to show, or when they start to feel the baby move inside them.

> The biggest fear that I'm having now is worrying if I'm going to be a good mother—if I'm going to be smart enough to even know when and how to feed the baby at the right times. And what about when my baby is in school? Being a teacher, I see how family life really affects them. I want to make the right

*choices as they're growing up, not spoil them. It's so easy to
look at someone and their kids and say, "I'm not going to be
that way." I don't want to be strict, but I don't want to be too
lenient either.*

—KRISTA

This fear of failure is often based on a woman's own experiences from
childhood—both good and bad. We grow up seeing our parents through
children's eyes.

*One time when I was young, I wanted to go get an ice cream
with my father and sister. He said I couldn't go. That was
one of those times that sticks, you know? I've always felt so
unacceptable, unworthy. But many years later, I talked to my
father about it, and he explained that on that particular day,
he needed to be alone with my sister to talk about some trouble
she was having at school. It had nothing to do with me.*

—ASHLEY

Sometimes all we need is a little context—the ability to understand
we're not the only ones who have lost our patience with kids.

*Last night my toddler was screaming. I don't know why,
because he can't—or he won't—talk yet. The phone was ring-
ing, supper was burning, and I'd had an awful day at work. So
I lost it. I screamed right back at him. Then I snatched him up
and put him in his crib and slammed the door. It made him
scream louder, and I just sat down and cried.*

—BRENDA

The first time a new mom experiences such a dramatic moment can be
frightening, especially if her family of origin is very dysfunctional. Moms
with more experience know that sometimes toddlers scream for no apparent reason, that being tired can shorten your fuse, and that separating
yourself from your child while you have a good cry may be the right
answer and the only way to survive. It doesn't make you a bad mom. The
next day you'll get the chance to do better.

Is Child-Free the Right Choice for Me?

When it comes to wondering whether or not you'll be a good mom, there is only one deal breaker: having an absolute aversion to children. If babies make you nervous, small children don't attract you, and dealing with teenagers makes you want to run screaming for the hills, then motherhood is probably not for you, no matter how much your partner longs for it or your family tells you that you'll be a great mom.

> We grew up very poor. We didn't have Pampers; we had diapers. One of my jobs was to clean diapers. I was nine or ten. I had three siblings in diapers. I remember dipping that diaper and thinking, "I am never gonna have kids, never gonna have kids—never!"
>
> —CAROLE

Short of an absolute aversion to children, there are other signs of what could be rocky times ahead if you decide to have children. None of these is insurmountable, and many women surprise themselves with how quickly and easily they adjust to motherhood, despite how concerned they were before the baby came.

If clutter just makes your skin crawl, you can pretty well wager that having an infant and a toddler is going to have your skin crawling into the next county. You'll need to learn to be flexible and cope in other ways.

If a good night's sleep is the most sacred event in your daily routine, then know that it's going to fall from the altar if you have a baby. You'll need to lower your expectations or get help from others in your home to protect your sleep.

If being in charge of the household schedule is most important to you, consider what your response will be when your teenager makes other plans for the same weekend you organized a family outing.

> *I am a very by-the-book sort of person. I don't have a lot of flexibility; I don't have a lot of tolerance for people doing things differently. I probably would not have tolerated all the things that children do—writing on the walls—well at all. In retrospect I say, "Boy, those kids would've been in a lot of trouble with this mom."*
>
> —DELORES

What if I Regret Having Children?

There will be times you do regret having children. While it's difficult for many women to admit, there is almost always one moment when a woman looks at her baby, young child, or teenager with doubt or regret. That doesn't make you evil; it makes you human.

There will also be times you feel like you just can't do it anymore. That's when you call on your partner, your parents, your in-laws, the local day care, your friends with children, your house of worship, or your next-door neighbor—someone to help so you can catch your breath and go back to doing it.

Occasionally, women in this situation feel so overwhelmed that they leave the household permanently but remain active in their child's lives. Margaret Sanger, the pioneer of birth control education in the early 1900s, was such a woman. Finding herself in an "apparently happy but confining marriage," she left her husband and children to pursue her own interests. While it can still be very difficult today to face the judgment of those who don't understand, some women have discovered that this solution is better not only for themselves but for their children. A woman who is in an abusive relationship with a man who is otherwise a good father, or who doesn't have the means to take her children with her, can leave the house and still play an important role in her children's lives from a safe distance. A woman who struggles with alcohol or drug dependency that is exacerbated by the stress of her children can spend shorter, healthier times with them. And a woman who can't find the support she needs and doesn't know what to do with her angry feelings can discover that the space provided by moving out can make her a happier person and a better mother on many other levels.

> *It was wonderful being the noncustodial parent. I could plan my time with them. We started having a lot more fun together. In fact, I was the fun parent because I was the noncustodial parent.*
>
> —CONNIE

> *Leaving them was the toughest decision I ever made. Tough enough without people thinking—and sometimes saying— what kind of mother was I? Well, I was the kind who loved her kids enough to know when to go. We're all happier now, and it can't matter what other people think.*
>
> —LANIE

What if I Regret Not Having Children?

There's a good possibility that if you decide not to have children, you will still experience moments when you wish you had. You may be surprised when that feeling strikes, and you may wonder if you did the right thing after all.

That's the time to take stock of your life, your love, and your family. You have made the decision after carefully considering the pros and cons. You have talked with people you trust, and you've read and heard the stories of women with and without children.

Of course, the decision about motherhood is often made with the heart, and there is a possibility your heart will change over time. If that becomes the case, you may want to allow yourself some time to mourn the loss you feel at that moment. Later, you can take steps to bring children into your life and have a lasting impact on them. While it isn't the same as having "your own," it can fill a void in your life that you have recognized.

> *A child-free friend of mine said she'd decided that if she had a child, at some point it would just become another person in her life. Maybe that's a good test. She has no regrets.*
>
> —MELISSA

Motherhood Is a Personal Choice.

Motherhood is a process of learning and growing, impossible to predict, an incredible journey of self-discovery, and the challenge of a lifetime.

Children can exceed our expectations and our wildest dreams and at times disappoint us bitterly. As parents, we can hope to instill some important, basic values in them. After that, it's all up for grabs as they grow into the people they were meant to be.

And if you remain child-free, you have a different but potentially just-as-exciting adventure awaiting you, with the option to share your life with children if you choose or to pursue the infinite possibilities that await you when you don't have the responsibility of motherhood.

The choice is yours.

Words of Wisdom

Select Quotes from Our Interviews and Surveys

Wait, wait, wait, until you are secure in yourself, until you have something to give that child. Don't expect anything from a child; they give nothing back, the little hoodlums! So many women think this child is going to love them. The child is going to love itself. You have to have the confidence to know that you will give what you must to your children. You have to be willing to sacrifice some of the time you need for yourself. You have to be prepared to give up a lot of your own dreams if you want to raise a child successfully.

Be prepared, but you don't need to wait until everything is perfectly aligned in your life to have children. If you want something enough, you'll find a way to make things work. Children are a lot of work, but they come with the biggest rewards.

Before you have a child with someone, take stock of that person's behavior. Are you already taking care of that person's every need? Does this person depend on you for almost everything? If so, have a baby with someone else, or have one by yourself. The last thing you need is to have two babies to take care of.

You can be wishy-washy about your own spiritual life, but when your own flesh and blood's life and future are on the line, you have to pick if you are going to live your faith or just give it lip service. My children deserve all my protection, love, and care. Nothing less.

Follow your heart, but you also have to really think about the conse-quences of it. It's a very difficult decision to make. You really have to think about what's best for everyone involved—you and the one you'll be responsible for the rest of your life. That's a big responsibility; it's forever.

It's a really tough decision. You have to feel it inside, really want to have one. It's not something for everybody. It's a very demanding and chal-lenging life that's unending, and that's a little scary.

If you want to have a child, don't wait on it. If you can act, you should act. In my age group, friends are having fertility problems. It's very dif-ficult, so difficult that some of them won't speak to me anymore. Then there are other women who just go on to other things.

It's not easy. There's always ups and downs. You should always love your child unconditionally, by being there every day for your child. If and when you decide to have a child, make sure you're ready.

Wait. Become a mother when you want to become a mother. It's differ-ent for everyone. It enlarges your life.

Look into your heart and ask yourself, can you really give that much of yourself for an extended period of time and still be able to come back and find that part of yourself that you've given away? Because at some point you're going to come back and see what you gave up. Can you do that and not be resentful, not be angry, and know you did it for a good reason?

If you decide to be child-free, you might be made to feel like you're inad-equate. You need confidence in yourself and belief in yourself that you can deal with it. You have to be strong.

You need a strong sense of who you are and what you want, and you have to be determined. Don't do it on a whim. Don't think that having a child is going to make your life complete. If you're looking for some-thing to complete your life, then you're not happy with yourself to begin with.

I would hope that women did some things in their lives, had some time for self-discovery before having children. I'm glad I had time to travel and the rewarding career and just growing as a person. So I would tell those women to be sure to have that time. Maybe not wait as long as I did. I think it makes me a better mom and a more well-rounded person.

Ask yourself how much you like children. If you do like them, then under what circumstances? When you walk into a restaurant or any other public place, do you say, "Oh great! There are kids here!"

Works Cited

Preface

Family Care International and the Safe Motherhood Inter-Agency Group, safemotherhood.org/facts_and_figures/unwanted_pregnancy.htm, March 2003.

Alan Guttmacher Institute figures as reported by Associated Press at ishipress.com/world-ab.htm, March 2003.

Chapter 2

Information on women marrying later: U.S. National Center for Health Statistics, *NVSR Bulletin*, 1990–1998. NVSR: Washington, D.C., 1999.

Infertility figures: Centers for Disease Control, "Total Fertility Rates and Birth Rates in the United States, 1940–1980," Portable Document Format file available at cdc.gov/nchs/data/statab/tab1x07p.pdf. Most recent as of 2003.

Chapter 4

Heidi Murkoff et al., *What to Expect When You're Expecting*, 3rd edition. New York: Workman Publishing, 2002.

Joanne Stone et al., *Pregnancy for Dummies*. Hoboken, N.J.: John Wiley and Sons, 1999.

Chapter 5

Data on women with children under five suffering disproportionate rate of mental health problems: Ian Brockington, *Motherhood and Mental Health*. Oxford: Oxford University Press, 1996.

Chapter 6

Divorce statistics: U.S. National Center for Health Statistics, *National Vital Statistics Reports*: cdc.gov/nchs/products/pubs/pubd/mvsr/supp/ 44-43/mvs43_9s.htm, 1990.

Stepmothering: James Bray and John Kelly, *Stepfamilies: Love, Marriage and Parenting in the First Decade* (New York: Broadway Books, 1999); and Ruth Webber, *Living in a Stepfamily* (Melbourne: Australia in Print, 1998).

Chapter 7

Hillary Rodham Clinton, *It Takes A Village and Other Lessons Children Teach Us*. New York: Simon and Schuster, 1999.

Data on grandparents as primary caretakers: U.S. Bureau of the Census, "Who's Minding the Kids? Grandparents Leading Childcare Providers," Census Bureau News, August 2002. Census Bureau website: census.gov/Press-release/www/2002/cb02-102.html.

Chapter 8

Data on fewer women having children: U.S. Census Bureau, "Population Profile of the U.S. 2000," Internet release 4-1, *Motherhood: The Fertility of American Women*, 2000.

Sylvia Ann Hewlett, *Creating a Life: Professional Women and the Quest for Children*. New York: Miramax, 2002.

Felice Schwartz with Jean Zimmerman, *Breaking with Tradition: Women and Work, The New Facts of Life*. New York: Warner Books, 1992.

Arlene Rossen Cardozo, *Sequencing: A New Solution for Women Who Want Marriage, Career, and Family*. New York: Atheneum Press, 1986.

Chapter 9

Costs of fertility treatments: Grand Rapids Fertility website (grandrapids fertility.com/successcostofivf.htm), 1997–1999 figures; The Fertility Institutes website (fertility-docs.com/fertility_fees.phtml), 2000 figure.

Information on cost: HCIA-Sachs provides health care payers, providers, employers, consultants, and pharmaceutical companies with relevant strategic intelligence. HCIA is a global enterprise with many variations on name. More information is available at solucient.com.

AFL-CIO press release, "Ask a Working Woman," May 2002 survey. Reported at aflcio.org/mediacenter/prsptm/pr05072002a.cfm.

U.S. Department of Agriculture, *Expenditure on Children by Families, 2001 Annual Report*, USDA website: usda.gov/cnpp/using2.htm.

One sperm bank willing to list prices online was Fairfax Cryobank (fairfaxcryobank.com), but there are others.

Projected college expenses: *Finaid!* Finaid Page, LLC: finaid.com/calculators/scripts/costprojector.cgi and finaid.com/calculators/savingsgrowth.phtml, March 2003.

Ann Crittenden, *The Price of Motherhood*. New York: Owl Books, 2001.

Chapter 10

Information on adoption: National Adoption Information Clearinghouse website: calib.com/naic, updated November 13, 2002.

Information on adoption subsidies offered by the federal government: North American Council on Adoptable Children (NACAC); National Adoption Assistance Training, Resource, and Information Network (NAATRIN); National Adoption Information Clearinghouse (calib.com/naic/parents/finan.cfm, updated November 2002). North American Council on Adoptable Children Adoption Subsidy Overview (nacac.org/adoptionsubsidy.html), July 2002.

Issues about the source and context of IVF success rates: Joseph D. Schulman, M.D., Genetics & IVF Institute (GIVF), "What's Your Success Rate? Understanding IVF Pregnancy Rate Statistics," Part I, March 19, 2003. GIVF website (givf.com).

Chapter 11

Data on the increase in single fathers: U.S. Census Bureau, "Families and Living Arrangements," March 2000: census.gov/population/www/socdemo/hh-fam.html.

Rosie Jackson, *Mothers Who Leave: Behind the Myth of Women Without Their Children* (New York: Rivers Oram Publishing, 1994).

Howard Zinn, *A People's History of the United States: 1492–Present*. New York: HarperCollins Publishers, 2001.

Resources

This is a partial list of resources, most of which we came across as we wrote the book and others that were referred to us. This list is not necessarily an endorsement for these organizations and books, only a sample of the information available.

ORGANIZATIONS AND WEBSITES

Adoption/Surrogacy

American Academy of Adoption Attorneys
P.O. Box 33053
Washington, DC 20033-0053
Phone: 202-832-2222
E-mail: trustees@adoptionattorneys.org

National network of adoption attorneys.

Growing Generations
Phone: 323-965-7500
Fax: 323-965-0900
E-mail: family@GrowingGenerations.com
Website: growinggenerations.com

California company that works with gay couples and surrogate mothers.

National Adoption Center
1500 Walnut St., Suite 701
Philadelphia, PA 19102
Phone: 800-TO-ADOPT
E-mail: nac@nationaladoptioncenter.org

Helps with referrals, information, and advocacy for children, focusing on minorities and children with special needs.

National Adoption Information Clearinghouse
U.S. Department of Health and Human Services
330 C St. SW
Washington, DC 20447
Phone: 703-352-3488 or 888-251-0075
Fax: 703-385-3206
E-mail: naic@calib.com

Includes information for all parties involved in adoption, adoption databases, and more complete information about current laws.

North American Council on Adoptable Children (NACAC)
970 Raymond Avenue, Suite 106
St. Paul, MN 55114
651-644-3036
Website: nacac.org

This organization staffs a hotline (800-470-6665) for parents, social workers, administrators, and lawyers who have specific questions about adoption assistance.

Costs

MSN Money
Website: http://moneycentral.msn.com

Features include USDA tables on costs of raising kids (http://moneycentral.msn.com/articles/family/kids/tlkidscost.asp) and a calculator for saving for college tuition (http://moneycentral.msn.com/investor/calcs/n_college/main.asp).

Financial Aid

FinAid Page
Website: finaid.org

This website is operated by FinAid Page, LLC. The site (available via either http://www.finaid.org or http://www.finaid.com) includes information on scholarships, loans, savings, and military aid. It has won awards from the College Board, the National Association of Student Financial Aid Administrators, the National Association of Graduate and Professional Students, and the American Institute for Public Service.

Career and Children

Catalyst
120 Wall St., 5th Floor
New York, NY 10005
Phone: 212-514-7600
Fax: 212-514-8470
Website: catalystwomen.org

A nonprofit research and advisory organization working to advance women in business.

Feminist Majority Foundation
1600 Wilson Blvd., Suite 801
Arlington, VA 22209
Phone: 703-522-2214
Fax: 703-522-2219
Website: feminist.org

A resource that leads to thousands of women's sites, including communities discussing women's life choices.

Mothers' Access to Careers at Home (MATCH)
P.O. Box 123
Annandale, VA 22003
Website: freestate.net/match

Organization for mothers who own a business or are starting one, designed to help mothers balance career and family.

Mothers and More
P.O. Box 31
Elmhurst, IL 60126
Phone: 630-941-3553
Fax: 630-941-3551
Website: mothersandmore.org

Support for women who decide to sequence—work, then raise children, then work again. Advocate for removing economic barriers to motherhood. Website offers a calculator for determining if you can afford to stay home.

National Association of At-Home Mothers
406 E. Buchanan Ave.
Fairfield, IA 52556
Website: athomemothers.com

Offers tips and a community of women discussing the move from career to staying at home, the effect on their relationships including with partner and friends, their self-esteem, and other issues.

Women's Bureau
U.S. Department of Labor
Website: dol.gov/wb

Information on career and job trends.

Child Care

Child Care Aware
1319 F St., NW, Suite 500
Washington, DC 20004
Phone: 800-424-2246
Website: childcareaware.org

Website has a search mechanism for finding a local "child care resource and referral" organization that will help you find qualified child care. Also lists tips for identifying good care.

International Nanny Association
900 Haddon Ave., Suite 438
Collingswood, NJ 08108-2101
Phone: 856-858-0808
Fax: 856-297-2519
Website: nanny.org

Nanny Network
Website: nannynetwork.com

Helps find agencies and nannies, provides an online community, offers articles on how to find and hire a nanny.

National Child Care Information Center
U.S. Department of Health and Human Services
Website: nccic.org

The "Questions" tab at the top of this website is particularly good for basic answers about cost and availability of child care and availability of federal and state programs to assist with cost. Beware, some information is dated.

For further information on day care, consult the National Foundation for Family Research and Education. A national registry of child-care providers is available through Care Connections, Inc. And on the Internet, a site that is designed for day-care providers but useful for parents as well is available at oursite.net/daycare/links.htm.

Child-Free Life

Childfree.net
Website: childfree.net

An extensive list of resources, including websites and books to support the child-free decision.

Childless by Choice
P.O. Box 695
Leavenworth, WA 98826
509-763-2112
Website: http://now2000.com/cbc

Clearinghouse for people who aren't having children or who are deciding about parenthood.

No Kidding!
Website: nokidding.net

Social groups organized around the country exclusively for people without children.

Dysfunction

Adult Children of Alcoholics
P.O. Box 3216
Torrance, CA 90510
Phone: 310-534-1815 (message only)
E-mail: meetinginfo@adultchildren.org (information on locating meetings)
E-mail: info@adultchildren.org (general information, meeting registrations, and other changes)

Al-Anon
1600 Corporate Landing Pkwy.
Virginia Beach, VA 23454-5617
Phone: 888-4AL-ANON

Support for family and friends of alcoholics.

Alcoholics Anonymous
Grand Central Station
P.O. Box 459
New York, NY 10163
Phone: 212-870-3400
Website: aa.org

Look for "Alcoholics Anonymous" in any telephone directory. In most urban areas, there is a central A.A. office, or "Intergroup."

American Counseling Association
5999 Stevenson Avenue
Alexandria, VA 22304-3300

Phone: 800-347-6647
Website: counseling.org

Free access to articles about specific issues important to consumers, answers to common questions about counseling, and guidance on how to find a professional counselor.

American Psychiatric Association
1000 Wilson Boulevard, Suite 1825
Arlington, VA 22209-3901
Phone: 703-907-7300
Website: psych.org

Information about a variety of psychiatric issues and disorders. Their site also features contact information for local APA chapters in the United States and Canada.

American Psychological Association (APA)
750 First Street, NE
Washington, DC 20002-4242
Phone: 800-374-2721
TDD/TTY: 202-336-5510
Website: apa.org

This site offers a "Consumer Help Center" with information on how to find help for life's problems and a referral service for finding a qualified psychologist in your area.

Narcotics Anonymous
P.O. Box 9999
Van Nuys, CA 91409
Phone: 818-773-9999
Fax: 818-700-0700

Survivors of Incest Anonymous
P.O. Box 190
Benson, MD 21018
Phone: 410-893-3322
Website: siawso.org

Infertility

American Infertility Association
666 Fifth Ave., Suite 278
New York, NY 10103
Phone: 888-917- 3777
Website: americaninfertility.org

Support groups, online chat and bulletin boards, physician referrals, fact sheets on infertility and adoption, and more.

American Society for Reproductive Medicine (ASRM)
1209 Montgomery Highway
Birmingham, AL 35216
Phone: 205-978-5000
Fax: 205-978-5005
Website: asrm.org

A voluntary nonprofit organization devoted to advancing knowledge and expertise in infertility, reproductive medicine, and biology. Their site offers answers to frequently asked questions about fertility and fertility options.

Centers for Disease Control

A federal agency dedicated to protecting people's health and providing information on health-related topics. Enter "assisted reproductive technology" into the site's search engine at cdc.gov. In addition, information on fertility clinic success rates and where to find clinics that participated in the 1999 national survey of assisted reproductive technology is available at cdc.gov/nccdphp/drh/ART99/index99.htm. Site updated August 6, 2002.

Genetics & IVF Institute
3020 Javier Road
Fairfax, VA 22031
Phone: 800-552-4363
Fax: 703-698-0418
Website: givf.com

The Genetics & IVF Institute describes itself as "the world's largest, fully integrated, specialized provider of infertility treatment and genetics services." This site provides amazingly up-to-date information for patients with infertility issues.

Internet Health Resources
1133 Garden Ln.
Lafayette, CA 94549
Phone: 925-284-9362
Website: ihr.com

Website includes an extensive listing of infertility resources, with information for patients, professionals, and providers.

Lesbian.org
Web site: lesbian.org/moms

Information on sperm banks and other issues related to lesbian parenting. Site is being maintained by Debbie Ranard, ranard@data.lib.udayton.edu, as of March 2003.

RESOLVE: The National Infertility Association
1310 Broadway
Somerville, MA 02144
Phone: 888-623-0744
Website: resolve.org

National group providing education, advocacy, and support for infertile couples, referral services, fact sheets. While the Resolve website lists fertility clinics, the list is in no way complete.

For an extensive list of worldwide infertility associations, go to Dr. Najeeb Layyous's website (updated March 2003) at layyous.com/infertility%20links/ infertility%20societies%20and%20organizations.htm

SpermDonorListing
Website: spermdonorlisting.com

A list of fourteen major sperm banks that agree to adhere to the guidelines of the American Society of Reproductive Medicine. Be sure to check the credentials of each bank. The website may not be up to date.

Motherhood

American Baby
110 Fifth Avenue
New York, NY 10011
Phone: 212-886-3600
Fax: 212-886-3648
Website: americanbaby.com

This site offers a variety of helpful resources for pregnant women and moms. Topics span preconception, pregnancy, baby, toddlers, and kids.

American College of Nurse-Midwives
818 Connecticut Ave., Suite 900
Washington, DC 20006
Phone: 202-728-9860
Fax: 202-289-9897
Website: midwife.org or acnm.org

Information for prospective patients and health care professionals about the nurse-midwife profession. Their site will also help you find an ACNM–affiliated nurse-midwife in your area.

American College of Obstetricians and Gynecologists (ACOG)
409 12th Street, SW
Washington, DC 20024
Phone: 202-638-5577
Website: acog.org

Information on a broad range of women's health topics, pregnancy, and postpartum conditions. Their site also helps you find an ACOG–affiliated ob-gyn physician anywhere in the world.

Association of Reproductive Health Professionals (ARHP)
2401 Pennsylvania Ave., NW, Suite 350
Washington, DC 20037
Phone: 202-466-3825
Fax: 202-466-3826
Website: arhp.org

Information about women's health and health providers; online brochures on calcium, contraceptives, and sexuality; and more.

Center for Reproductive Law & Policy
120 Wall St.
New York, NY 10005
Phone: 917-637-3600
Fax: 917-637-3666
Website: crlp.org

An international advocacy group supporting the rights of women to control their own health care choices.

MSN Family
Website: http://family.msn.com

Occasional articles for couples considering parenthood, but mostly useful if you're already pregnant.

National Abortion Federation
1755 Massachusetts Ave., NW, Suite 600
Washington, DC 20036
Phone: 202-667-5881
Website: prochoice.org

The professional association of abortion providers in the United States and Canada. Provides political and medical information, as well as an abortion provider search function on its website.

Parenting.com
Website: parenting.com

Includes recent articles on adoption, infertility, parenting of different ages. Also includes calculators for just about any parenting-related subject.

Planned Parenthood Federation of America
810 Seventh Ave.
New York, NY 10019
Phone: 212-541-7800
Fax: 212-245-1845
Website: plannedparenthood.org

Information on how to have a healthy pregnancy; how to talk to teens about pregnancy; women's health; how, when, and where to get an abortion; political action; and more.

Safetyforum Research
P.O. Box 470
Arlington, VA 22210-0470
703-469-3700
Website: safetyforum.com

Information and updates on safety standards and recalls can be found on Safety-Forum's website at safetyforum.com, which also has discussion forums and a search mechanism so you can look up a particular product.

Single Mothers by Choice
P.O. Box 1642, Gracie Square Station
New York, NY 10028
Phone: 212-988-0993
E-mail: mattes@pipeline.com

Primarily single women in their thirties or forties who have either decided to have or are considering having children outside of marriage.

BOOKS

Work and Motherhood

Bayalick, Maria, and Linda Saslow. *The Three Career Couple: Mastering the Art of Juggling Work, Home, and Family*. Princeton, N.J.: Peterson's Guides Publishing, 1993.

Belsky, Jay, and John Kelly. *The Transition to Parenthood: How a First Child Can Change a Marriage*. New York: Delacorte Press, 1995.

Holcomb, Betty. *Not Guilty! The Good News About Working Mothers*. New York: Scribner's and Sons, 1998.

Lerner, Harriet. *The Mother Dance: How Children Change Your Life*. New York: HarperCollins, 1998.

Peters, Joan. *Not Your Mother's Life: Changing the Rules of Work, Love and Family*. Cambridge, Mass.: Perseus Books, 2001.

———. *When Mothers Work*. Cambridge, Mass.: Perseus Books, 1998.

Williams, Joan. *Unbending Gender: Why Family and Work Conflict and What to Do About It.* New York: Oxford University Press, 2000.

Child-Free Choice

Bartlett, Jane. *Will You Be a Mother? Women Who Choose to Say No.* New York: NYU Press, 1995.

Brady, Joan. *I Don't Need a Baby to Be Who I Am: Thoughts and Affirmations.* New York: Pocket Books, 1998.

Burkett, Elinor. *The Baby Boon: How Family-Friendly America Cheats the Childless.* New York: The Free Press, 2000.

Cain, Madelyn. *The Childless Revolution: What It Means to Be Childless Today.* Cambridge, Mass.: Perseus Books, 2002.

Casey, Terri. *Pride and Joy: The Lives and Passions of Women Without Children.* Hillboro, Ore.: Beyond Words Publishing, 1998.

Lang, Susan. *Women Without Children: The Reasons, the Rewards, the Regrets.* Avon, Mass.: Adams Media Corporation, 1996.

Ratner, Rochelle, ed. *Bearing Life: Women's Writings on Childlessness.* New York: The Feminist Press, 2000.

Safer, Jeanne. *Beyond Motherhood: Choosing a Life Without Children.* New York: Pocket Books, 1996.

Dysfunction

Brown, Nina. *Children of the Self-Absorbed: A Grown-Up's Guide to Getting Over Narcissistic Parents.* Oakland, Calif.: New Harbinger Publications, 2001.

Farmer, Steven. *Adult Children of Abusive Parents: A Healing Program for Those Who Have Been Physically, Sexually, or Emotionally Abused.* New York: Ballantine Books, 1990.

Forward, Susan. *Toxic Parents: Overcoming Their Hurtful Legacy and Reclaiming Your Life.* New York: Bantam Doubleday Dell, 2002.

Neuharth, Dan. *If You Had Controlling Parents: How to Make Peace with Your Past and Take Your Place in the World.* New York: HarperCollins Cliff Street Books, 1999.

Woititz, Janet Geringer. *Adult Children of Alcoholics.* Deerfield Beach, Fla.: Health Communications, 1990.

Other

Barrett, Nina. *I Wish Someone Had Told Me: A Realistic Guide to Early Motherhood*. Chicago: Academy Chicago Press, 1997.

Bombardieri, Merle. *The Baby Decision: How to Make the Most Important Decision of Your Life*. New York: Rawson, Wade, 1981.

Crittenden, Ann. *The Price of Motherhood*. New York: Henry Holt and Company, Metropolitan Books, 2001.

Engel, Beverly. *The Parenthood Decision: Deciding Whether You Are Ready and Willing to Become a Parent*. New York: Doubleday, 1998.

Maushart, Susan. *The Mask of Motherhood: How Becoming a Mother Changes Everything and Why We Pretend It Doesn't*. New York: Penguin Books, 2000.

Swigert, Jane. *The Myth of the Bad Mother*. New York: Doubleday, 1991.

Wolf, Naomi. *Misconceptions: Truth, Lies, and the Unexpected on the Journey to Motherhood*. New York: Doubleday, 2001.

Index